# GODLY

## *Marriage*

### *and*

# FAMILY LIFE

---

## J.O.Y. ALADETAN

**ARPress**
45 Dan Road Suite 36
Canton MA 02021

Hotline: 1(800) 220-7660
Fax:    1(855) 752-6001


Ordering Information:
Quantity sales. Special discounts are available on quantity purchases by corporations, associations, and others. For details, contact the publisher at the address above.

Printed in the United States of America.

| ISBN-13: | Paperback | 979-8-89389-397-7 |
| --- | --- | --- |
| | Hardcover | 979-8-89389-399-1 |
| | eBook | 979-8-89389-398-4 |

Library of Congress Control Number: 2024916685

# Praise for *Godly Marriage and Family Life*

This book, *Godly Marriage and Family Life*, is a blessing to the body of Christ and a guide for anyone who wants to fulfil God's purpose for marriage and family. It is my prayer that the Lord will make it a huge success, in Jesus's name.

Pastor Leke Sanusi
RCCG Victory House
London, UK

As a member of the C and S fold, I believe a person can only be bold enough to write such a book in such detail if the person is walking with God. As a person yet to be married, I smiled happily whilst reading this book, as it was to me just a reminder of how my marriage life will become a very successful one, in Jesus's name.

I appreciated the way you emphasised to those that have sinned along the way in their marriage life that hope is not lost; they can repent, ask for forgiveness, and then go and sin no more.

It was just amazing how you ended the book with a number of prayer points for married and unmarried readers alike. God bless you, sir.

Sister Toyin Idowu
C and S Headquarters
Earlham Grove, London.

This book is an X-ray through research from the laboratory of homemaking. Mr Aladetan has sacrificially produced this book as a result of his high esteem for the ideal life that is God's total plan for man. It is indeed an indispensable reference for marriage counsellors, pastors, and all who aspire for maximum peace in every home. This book receives our highest recommendation.

Rev Williams Ade Oyekan
Christ Christian College
Lagos, Nigeria

This book on marriage and family life addresses a relevant problem, gives useful and pragmatic suggestions, and provides detailed scriptural information that can help the married and unmarried alike in their desire for the instruction of Christian family ideas and norms.

Prof. Rev. Dapo Asaju
Dept of Religions
Lagos State University
Lagos, Nigeria

This book states for the enquirer on how to predicate one's marriage and family on a foundation that cannot be moved. This foundation is Jesus Christ. It offers a panacea to one of the greatest ills of our age. This book is God's gift to our generation, and therefore it should be bought for consumption and regular refilling of the Spirit of God in the family.

Pastor Gideon O. Oyedepo
C and S Bible Ministries
Lagos, Nigeria

# THE VISION FOR THIS BOOK

This book was envisioned for the renewal of the family values intended by God for every society. God is a family God (Rev. 21: 3–4). I prayerfully ask Him to quicken this vision with His Spirit, in Jesus's name:

1. For the healing of every troubled marriage
2. To reconcile every broken marriage
3. To bring about family values in our societies
4. To raise heavenly kingdom families on earth

Marriage is the crowning work of creation, a foundation for life. God blessed and gave dominion to humankind to rule over the earth. Marriage is God's invention, so it is sacred. God saw the need for it (Gen. 2: 18) and invented it (Gen. 2: 22–24). Marriage is the first government and the first church on earth. It existed before human culture, tradition, religion, and civilization were developed. It is a platform for perfect communion and fellowship with God and a context where God wants men and women to be like Him. Marriage is a seed of life. When planted in good soil, it grows to produce good fruit. If it is planted on bad soil, it will produce bad seeds, cause defects, and contaminate lives. It is time to celebrate God with our marriages and bring about family values in our societies.

God has existed from eternity past without beginning; everything begins in Him. The Triune God is forever a united and indivisible body. One way to imagine it is that the Father is the body of the Godhead, the Son is the soul of the Godhead, and the Holy Spirit is, not surprisingly, the spirit of the Godhead; "they are one indivisible" (Deut. 6:4). Together, they brought the perfect creation into existence (Gen. 1: 1–3); together, they created man in their image and likeness (Gen. 1: 26); together, they brought salvation to mankind. The Father gave the Son (John 3: 16), the Son gave His life, and the Son sent the Holy Spirit as promised by the Father (Acts 2: 1–4). Therefore, God expects all ideal marriages to be united in body, soul, and spirit until the end, to reflect His likeness.

Knowing Jesus, the personification of truth, will set you free. The devil has come to steal, kill, and destroy (John 10: 10). Only the husbands and wives who allow the Good Shepherd to captain their marriages can fly higher and land successfully to the end. Without Jesus Christ, we can do nothing (John 15: 5). Adam recognized that his wife was bone of his bone and flesh of his flesh; hence, he celebrated his marriage. Jesus commands that what God has joined together, let no man put asunder (Matt. 19: 6).

Let us therefore arise to restore to our societies the family values that are gradually fading away.

# Contents

# Foreword

The world today is grappling with the consequences of faulty family values practised by past generations. God cherishes the family unit, but modern civilisation, especially in the West, has gradually defiled the institution of marriage and encouraged divorce and single parenting. This has decreased respect in the home and driven God out of classrooms, removing God's word from school curricula. The shocking result is a moral vacuum and the breakdown of law and order in many ramifications.

This unfortunate situation calls for the writing of a book like this to rescue Christian families from a downward slide. J.O.Y Aladetan's book, *Christian Marriage and Family Life,* addresses a relevant problem, gives useful and pragmatic suggestions, and provides delightful scriptural information to help married and unmarried persons alike in their desire for instruction about Christian families. I pray that this book will serve as a tool to protect the institution of marriage and Christian families and that it will promote and enlarge the kingdom of God.

**Professor Dapo Asaju**
Department of Religions,
Lagos State University, Lagos, Nigeria

# Preface

The first institution established by God at creation was the marriage institution. Jesus, God incarnate, supported the formation and foundation of the institution when he made it the place of His first miracle, in Cana of Galilee, by making sweet wine from water in pitchers. Jesus added joy, gladness, and happiness to the marriage institution for all who tasted the wine He made available at the wedding ceremony.

This implies that marriage is about togetherness, a union where the couple should reign from its beginning to end, till death do them part. This book is not just an appropriate reminder of the implications of the climbing rate of divorces of marriages performed in churches; it also provides ways for couples to maintain oneness in Christ when they are filled with the Holy Spirit and possess Christ-centred natures, as directed in 1 John 1: 7.

The members of a couple are meant to complement each other and not compete among themselves, no matter what the disparities are in their lives. Once they have made their choice prayerfully, confirmed by the Holy Spirit, they ought to make their marriage survive all periods of conflicts.

The author has deep concerns for the institution of marriage and lists out some potential areas of conflict. If the offered solutions are heeded, divorce may be avoided. The author's advice comes from both his own marriage experience and his experience as a minister of God. He has joined many couples in holy matrimony, and he provides biblical marriage counselling, guidance and advice.

We therefore recommend this book to all young couples: the ones who are about to be married as well as those whose marriages are challenging and look like they are on the brink of collapse. All married and successful couples are also advised to read this book to strengthen and uphold their marriages through its practical guidance on leading a Christian married life.

### Pastors Margaret and Joseph Gono

This book is dedicated to God Most High, in appreciation of His love, for creating man in His own image and likeness, and for His establishment of the marriage institution as the first church and human government on earth. I also dedicate this book to His only begotten Son, our Lord Jesus Christ, who came to this world and performed the miracle of turning water to wine as a symbol of restoring the marriage institution, and who, ultimately, offered Himself as a living sacrifice on the cross at Calvary to redeem the world.

I dedicate this book to the Holy Spirit for imparting the wisdom, knowledge, and understanding for me to write this must-read book. Also, this book is dedicated to Christian families all over the world, who are 'the co-heirs with the Lord'. This book is dedicated to the memory of my late parents, "Lady and Pa Aladetan, who laid my feet on the path of the cross before they departed this sinful world, and to my family living and yet unborn. Lastly, I dedicate this book to the ministers of God all over the world.

# Acknowledgements

I want to thank those who in one way or the other rendered assistance to me in preparation of this book. I commend the Holy Spirit for an impartation of knowledge and wisdom to write this book. My appreciation goes to my family for their support and encouragement. I thank Professor Dapo Asaju, who wrote the foreword, and Pastors Margaret and Joseph Gono for the preface. I also want to thank Brother Wilson Mbakweni and Brother Jones Martins, who proofread and Sister Yinka Esan, who helped in typesetting the first edition. My appreciation goes to friends and well-wishers who contributed financially to the production of this book. I thank Brother Sahr Gandi Capio for encouragement.

I must express my appreciation to my late wife of twenty-seven years, Taiwo Aladetan who taught me confidentiality and perseverance in marriage before she went to rest in the Lord; she was the rock of our marriage – a mother, a sister, a friend, and indeed a wife. May her gentle soul rest in perfect peace. I also acknowledge my beautiful and lovely daughter, Mrs E. Olayinka Aladetan-Akinola, for her dynamism.

# Author's Prayers

As I write this book, I confess every sin that I committed before and during my marriage and the sins of my parents and my ancestors before and during their marriages. I pray that God will forgive me and the past generations in my family for every marital sin committed. Father, cleanse me and my generation with the blood of Jesus Christ so that our sins will not be remembered. Amen.

I also immerse all the readers of this book in the blood of Jesus Christ for total cleansing from the sins of fornication and adultery. They must make it to heaven; none among them will perish with the world. Amen.

I cover the world with the precious blood of Jesus for total cleansing and redemption of souls from the sins of sexual perversion that have plagued society. Father Lord, the world is spiritually blind to your heart for the marriage institution, which you institutionalised for your glory and for the blessing of humanity. God, heal the world of this spiritual sickness and bring sanity into Christian homes, in Jesus's name, amen.

I pray for God's guidance for the coming generations that have yet to take the giant step of marriage. Father, give them hearts of true love and give them your Spirit to obey your word. Bind them together with divine love and truth as they take the flesh of their flesh and bone of their bones to the altar for an everlasting covenant marriage, in Jesus's name, amen.

Father Lord, let your name be glorified in the lives of the readers of this book. I pray that their descendants will be established as a source of eternal glory; little among them will become thousands, a mighty and powerful nation. Their marriages will be established with love, truth, peace, and the joy of the Lord will reign in their hearts forever, in Jesus's name, amen.

# Introduction

Marriage is a platform established by God for human being to be blessed, fruitful, and dominate the earth.

Genesis chapter 1 narrates the chronological order of creation, whilst chapter 2 focuses on the creation of man from the dust of the ground and the creation of woman from the rib of Adam to establish the marriage institution (Gen. 2: 18–24).

Marriage is God's idea and initiative; He saw the need and made the provisions for it, having provided the most comfortable environment and the logistics for the would-be first couple. God said: "It is not good for a man to be alone; I will make a helper suitable for him" (Gen. 2: 18).

The companionship of marriage is clearly the heart of God for human beings, whom He created in His image and likeness. Adam was not responsible for any work of creation, including the establishment of the marriage institution. Marriage is the revelation of the incomprehensible love of God for humans, showing that He knows our needs beyond our understanding.

Therefore, marriage is the first church and the first government on earth; it transcends culture, tradition, religion, and civilisation. It was designed to be the extension of Triune God on earth.

Marriage is a spiritual fusion of two bodies becoming one flesh, united as one body, soul, and spirit till the end of one spouse's life. This mystery needs to be studied, understood, respected, and sustained.

*Chapter One*

# THE GIFT OF GOD FOR HUMANITY

### Foundation of Life

The kingdom of God is not a democratic setting but a theocratic rule, and God's sovereign authority is supreme over all the created orders, both in heaven and on earth. God spoke, and the fullness of heaven and earth came into existence and are sustained. The Bible says: "The earth is the Lord's and the fullness therein, the world and all who live in it" (Ps. 24: 1).

As a minister of God, I tenaciously believed in the supremacy of the spoken word of God with which God created the hosts of heaven and the earth.. (Genesis 1:1-3; Colossians 1:16-17), I also

1

believed that God lives in His Word to rule over all creation. and the word is God. (John 1:3) I also like to record it that all creations in heaven and the earth are the products of the word of God, 'devil and human inclusive'.

The mystery of marriage, as instituted by God, goes beyond human knowledge and understanding; it is indeed spiritual and needs to be well-understood by every human, particularly Christians. Godly or Christian marriage is the finishing product of Elohim, a perfect institution established to perfectly represent the Triune God on earth, followed by releasing dominion to the couple to rule and replenish the earth.

Before God moulded the dust of the ground to form man and establish the institution of marriage as the crowning work of creation, darkness and water covered the earth. God sent the light to subdue darkness and then separated water from the land so it could produce vegetation and fruits. In same manner, this book is intended to shed light into the marriage institution, established by God but now obscured with various cultural and traditional practices.

Let me give further insights into the uniqueness of marriage institution in relation to all creatures, the beast, the birth, the snakes, fishes include ants etc. are created to procreate and increase but never married or have nuclear family but only human does.

God began when he expresses his love for the lonely man (Adam) that it is not good for man to be alone (Genesis 2:18) God went further to perform the first surgical operation when he removed a bone from the rib of Adam to create a suitable and desirous helpmate and presented Eve to Adam. Genesis 2:20-22) and Adam celebrated Eve as 'the bone of my bone and the flesh of my flesh' and called her a womb-man (v23) then, God joined the first couple together in marriage to establish the marriage institution. 'Therefore shall a man leave his father and his mother, and shall cleave unto his wife and they shall be on flesh. (Genesis 2:24). This was the first Church, first government upon which God releases jurisdictional power for man to rule the earth. (Genesis 1:28)

Strong and stable marriages and families are the bedrock of a stable and successful society. It is my conviction that only a return to traditional family values, as instituted by God, can provide this strong foundation. The undermining of this institution has had disastrous consequences in the lives of families and in society in general. Marriage, as an institution, should be taught as a subject in institutions of higher learning worldwide, particularly theological colleges should produce degree holders in marriage counselling and administration in order to manage this honourable institution. Also, the church as a whole needs to gird her loins and rise to restore sanctity into the marriage institution and into society so that the world will continue to enjoy the peace and full blessings of God.

Some people are trading the foundational values of life, such as marriage, for the premises of modern life. Marriage, which was ordained by God, transcends cultures, traditions, religions, and civilisation. God saw the need for marriage and established it as a crowning work of creation with a precise rule: "For this reason a man will leave his father and mother and be united to his wife and they shall become one flesh" (Gen. 2: 24 NIV). Upon this foundation, God pronounced blessings and released man to rule over the earth. Therefore, marriage also must be ruled with the fear of God and total obedience to His sovereign law.

The Bible says: "The law of the Lord is perfect reviving the soul. The statutes of the Lord are trustworthy making wise the simple. The precepts of the Lord are right giving joy to the heart. The commands of the Lord are radiant giving light to the eyes. The fear of the Lord is pure enduring forever. The ordinances of the Lord are sure and altogether righteous they are more precious than gold than much pure gold. They are sweeter than honey, than honey from the comb. By them is your servant warned us, keeping them there is great reward" (Ps. 19: 7–11 NIV).

As mentioned in the introduction, marriage is the first church and the first government on earth in which God expects His precepts to be obeyed in order to bring everlasting blessing, prosperity, and perfection on earth. In like manner, the church was established on the day of Pentecost as God's divine law-enforcing agency, mandated to enforce God's laws on earth and to prepare mankind for the second coming of our Lord Jesus Christ, who will usher believers into the kingdom of God as written (John 14: 1–3; Rev. 21: 1–6).

As stated previously, Christianity is theocratic, meaning rules for life flow from the heart of God and are established by our Lord Jesus Christ for the redeemed, obedient children of God (Acts 11: 19–26). Godly or Christian marriage is a sacred union between a man and a woman who are destined for an eternal glory that transcends cultures, traditions, civilisation, and religion to establish God's perfect will on earth. The Bible says: "Heaven and earth will pass away but my words will never pass away" (Matt. 24: 35 NIV).

Christianity teaches faithfulness, chastity, sacredness, one-flesh union, and permanence in marriage. But many traditions and cultures, including Western civilisation, teach and encourage promiscuity, polygamy, and repression of women in marriage and in society in general. Some religions allow unfaithfulness, polygamy, and repression of women, whilst civilisation encourages and promotes sexual perversion, divorce, single parenthood, and pornography. This book will focus on the heart of God for the marriage institution that He established for His children and for the blessing of mankind, not the concept of marriage according to human ideals.

I came from a humble background where polygamy was freely practiced. The number of wives you had determined your influence in society and indicated how wealthy you were. I did not come from a polygamous house, but I came from a broken home and never enjoyed the affection of parents with a united marriage. I was born into a Christian religious sect where polygamy is not prohibited. I was also raised by a Muslim family friend who loved and treated me as one of his sons; he encouraged me to practice Islam during my youth, and I did for seven years.

My background influenced me to expect that I would eventually practice polygamy. I almost fell into this trap before I met Christ. Surprisingly, God had warned me never to be unfaithful to any woman even before I got married. My mind was troubled each time I considered the discrepancy between my background and God's commands. I began to wonder why God would single me out among my family members and ask me not to marry more than one wife. It never occurred to me that God was preparing me for pastoral and evangelical responsibilities. I became rebellious towards God and struggled with the temptation to fulfil my desires; I thought it would work for me instead of following God. I always found myself in trouble until I met Christ in 1989 and enrolled in C&S College of Divinity and Seminary, Lagos Nigeria.

God began to reveal to me the secret of marriage and why He did not allow me to fall into the trap of a polygamy system of marriage. When I met Christ, I began to regret my unfaithfulness at the initial stage of my marriage. The truth that I knew eventually set me free; I repented, confessed, and asked God to forgive me. Without a doubt, He has forgiven me and washed me with His blood.

My encounter with Jesus Christ challenged me to break loose from the foundational errors of my generation and prepared me to write this book, *Godly Marriage and Family Life*, to help others to do the same. I pray that this book will heal every troubled marriage and restore broken homes all over the world. I hope that it prepares the present and coming generations for perfect marital lives, fulfilling God's glory and blessing in every marriage and family.

As the world is grappling with the problems of the sexual revolution and promoting immoral sodomitic practices that are gradually destroying the foundational values of life, Satan and his demons have taken advantage of this trend to gain more legal ground to invade marriages, homes, families, and human lives. The devil has also afflicted humanity with incurable illnesses, like venereal diseases, including HIV. He is bent, desperately destroying marriages and families and depriving many of eternal life throughout the world.

Some wealthy male Christians around the world, including some ministers of God, are tempted to get divorced or enjoy having physical relationships with women other than their wives, but they regard their wives as subjects who must not get involved in extramarital affairs. It is true that a woman's husband having an affair doesn't give her permission to be unfaithful. However, has

God given any man the permission to get involved in extramarital affairs? The answer is no. This reminds me of a story of a woman in the Bible who was brought to Jesus for committing adultery. According to the law of Moses, such an offence carried the capital punishment of stoning the criminal to death, but Jesus knew the hypocrisy in the hearts of her accusers. I imagine that as He meditated before responding, He must have been thinking: *after all, sexual offences involve two persons. Where is the male offender?*

Jesus then demanded that anyone among her accusers who had not committed sin should be the first to cast a stone (John 8: 1–11). What is not good for John is equally not good for Joanne. Adultery, the only reason allowed by the law of Moses in the Old Testament to issue a certificate of divorce, is a curse for humanity and must be avoided. Read and meditate on 1 Corinthians 6: 9–10, Galatians 5: 19–21 and Revelation 21: 8.

It is evident in Europe and America and other advanced societies that marriage, as defined and instituted by God, is diminishing by the day, and this has resulted in a breakdown of law and order.

## Origin of Marriage

Marriage began in the garden of Eden long before the culture, tradition, religion, and civilisation we are familiar with today. It is an idea from God, provided as a foundation for life's journey from birth to eternity upon which blessing and prosperity are laid and dominion is given to man (Gen. 1: 28 NIV). When properly planted in good soil, it is a seed that grows to become a tree that produces good fruit, but if planted in bad soil, it will produce bad seeds of infection in people's lives.

Marriage is not a human invention or a social custom; it was initiated by God. As stated previously, God saw man's need for companionship in the garden of Eden, and He instituted marriage. God said, "It is not good that man should be alone" (Gen. 2: 18). He carried it out like a father giving away his daughter to her bridegroom at the altar; the Lord God brought her to the man (see Gen. 2: 22) as a precedent for marriage throughout time and commanded that:

> Therefore a man shall leave his father and mother and be joined to his wife, and they shall become one flesh. (Gen. 2: 24)

When our Lord Jesus Christ referred to marriage in Matthew 19: 4–6, as did the Apostle Paul in Ephesians 5: 31, they made the point that marriage has been ordained by God, therefore, humans do not have the right to do as they like with it. "Haven't you read 'he replied, that at the beginning the Creator made them male and female, and said, for this reason a man will leave his father and mother and be united to his wife, and the two will become one flesh so they are no longer two but one. Therefore, what God has joined together let man not separate" (Matt. 19: 4–6).

Since marriage was instituted by God, the authority governing the institution remains the word of God, as expressly stated in scripture:

> So God created man in His own image and likeness, in the image of God created he him male and female created he them. And God blessed them and God said unto them, be fruitful and multiply, and replenish the earth and subdue it, and have dominion over the fish of the sea and over the fowl of the air and over every living things that moves upon the earth. (Gen. 1: 27–28)

Scripture makes it clear that humans are the only creature made in the image and likeness of God, and we are to rule over all other creatures and to replenish the earth. This is God's motivating factor for the establishment of the marriage institution. God's provision of a helpmate to Adam in the garden of Eden was because of His passionate love for Adam and to break the loneliness of life. This first, perfect marriage was also meant to establish God's ordinances of blessing, fruitfulness, replenishment, and the power for humans to rule over the earth.

The Triune God – the Father, the Son, and the Holy Spirit – created the heavens and the earth and was sole manager of the universe, including man, before the establishment of marriage. Since there was no suitable partner amongst other creatures for Adam, God performed the first surgical operation to draw out a bone from Adam's rib to create Eve, the mother of all humanity "And the rib which the Lord God had taken from the man made him a woman and brought unto the man (Adam). And Adam said this is now the bone of my bones and the flesh of my flesh, she shall be called woman because she was taken out of man" (Gen. 2: 21–23).

Without a doubt, the creation of heaven and earth was perfect, as declared by God in Genesis 1: 31, but the creation of woman reinforces the overall perfection of creation. God's statement that it was not good for man to be alone in Genesis 2: 18 suggests that man is not complete without a woman, and replenishment of the earth is not possible without a woman. Likewise, a woman without a man in her life through marriage is a deficiency of life. Therefore, marriage was designed to meet the basic need of God's creation, so people could experience love and companionship. This is a perfect description of the relationship which God intended between husband and wife, because of their compatibility, to have a one-flesh union till the end of one of their lives.

Men and women are ordained to marry for the following reasons: (a) to replenish the earth for the work of dominion, (b) to establish a one-flesh union that takes priority over all family relationships, and (c) to represent that marriage is a crowning work of creation, a higher institution of learning for how to manage two joint bodies, made one by God. God is the Pro-chancellor of this divine institution; all students remain under-graduate till eternity.

Adam celebrated God's gift of a wife to him as he exclaimed, "This is now bone of my bone and flesh of my flesh, she shall be called woman, for she was taken out of my rib" (Gen. 2: 23). A declaration made by God follows immediately: "For this reason, a man will leave his father and mother and be united to his wife and they will become one flesh" (Gen. 2: 24). This is supposed to be the ideal focus of Godly or Christian Marriage until death do them part, as written in scripture.

My research reveals that marital dissolution is not as common in Middle Eastern and Asian nations as it is in the West and other nations where Christianity is thriving. Could this rampant divorce rate be a result of rejecting God's law or abusing the grace of God? It's very sad to see the nations that pioneered spreading the gospel globally are now tolerating promiscuity, divorce, and single parenting instead of promoting united parenting to enhance family values.

## One-Flesh Union

God's idea of a one-flesh union for marriage emanated from the concept of the Trinity. God the Father, the Son, and the Holy Spirit are one indivisible God. The Triune God was united in eternity past to create heaven and earth and participated jointly in the work of salvation to restore humanity back to paradise.

God the Father gave His Son (John 3: 16), God the Son gave His life and sent the Holy Spirit (John 16: 7; Acts 2: 2–4) to abide in and perfect believers and to edify the church. Marriage, then, was established by God as an extension of the Trinitarian Godhead; the husband and the wife are joined together in body, soul, and spirit, whilst the children of the marriage are expected to be united in all spheres of life with their parents until eternity.

Becoming one flesh means to exhibit faithfulness in spiritual, mental, emotional, and sexual interaction in order to establish a bond that is more than physical. The one-flesh union establishes a bond of personhood in love, truth, peace, joy, patience, endurance, perseverance, faithfulness, forgiveness, and tolerance (Gal. 5: 22–24) which is fundamental to the permanence of marriage.

The one-flesh union does not destroy the personhood of either partner; it celebrates the unity of two people giving themselves to each other in love, truth and forgiveness. This concept has a spiritual quality and symbolises the depth of the marriage relationship as a reflection of the Triune God.

The one-flesh union establishes divine strength needed by couples to implement and accomplish the work of dominion, leading to a perfect manifestation of blessing, fruitfulness, prosperity and replenishment of the earth. To state it plainly, an unfaithful husband or wife cannot lead a church into righteousness; also, maritally unfaithful political leaders cannot lead a nation into prosperity. I will explain more of this concept throughout the book. Remember, the marriage institution was the first church and the first government on earth.

The scripture emphasises that unfaithfulness in marriage is an abomination to church leadership. For example, it is written:

> Here is a trustworthy saying. If anyone sets his
> heart on being an overseer, he desires a noble task.
> Now the overseer must be above reproach. The

husband of but one wife, temperate, self-controlled, respectable, hospitable, able to teach. (1 Tim. 3: 1–2)

The one-flesh union demands that both husband and wife regard their marriage as God's honourable estate, not meant to be broken. It also means that each spouse in a marriage is obliged to practise respect and to maintain confidentiality, preventing undue interference by any third parties.

The marriage contract at the garden of Eden marked the crowning work of God's perfect creation, which caused God to release His blessings and give authority to man. The Bible says, "So God created man in his own image, in the image of God he created him; male and female he created them. God blessed them and said to them, 'Be fruitful and increase in number; fill the earth and subdue it. Rule over the fish of the sea and the birds of the air and over every living creature that moves on the ground'" (Gen. 1: 27–28).

Sexual union between a man and woman in marriage is therefore a lawful, honourable, and sanctifying act of consummating marriage. All married couples must observe it with the right intent. But without the bonds of marriage, sexual indulgence is a debasing sin, abominable in the sight of God. The Apostle Paul wrote about this, saying, "Do you not know that the unrighteous will not inherit the kingdom of God? Do not be deceived. Neither fornicators, nor idolaters, nor adulterers, nor homosexuals nor sodomites nor thieves, nor covetous, nor drunkards, nor revellers, nor extortionists will inherit the kingdom of God" (1 Cor. 6: 9–10).

The big questions are: did God command one man and two women, or a man with a man, or a woman with a woman to become one flesh, and can one man truly become one flesh with two women? Since the scripture shows that God created a woman as the helper suitable to the man and prescribed that a man will leave his father and mother and be united to his wife and they shall become one flesh (Genesis 2: 24), the answer is no. If the answer is no, then polygamy, lesbianism, and homosexuality are against the will of God for Godly or Christian marriage.

## Helpmate

A helpmate, in God's terms, is the union of a man and a woman joined together in holy matrimony as one indivisible body, soul, and spirit to share a common vision of life and destiny together until death parts them.

The two are joined together in common thought for blessing, fruitfulness, and increase with a dominion mandate to rule over the earth. This is similar to the popular English saying, behind every successful man, there is a woman; she is called a helpmate. She is not a slave but a virtuous woman, treated by her husband with love, respect, and honour. The whole of creation is good, but the creation of women reinforces the overall goodness of what was created. God intended for marriage to meet the basic human needs of love and companionship, through each spouse having a helpmate equal to him- or herself and sharing life responsibilities together as mates, not as master and servant.

## Marriage Is Meant to Be Heterosexual

In the beginning, God provided for Adam a woman, not another man; God did not join Eve together with another woman, either. Nowadays, homosexual and lesbian marriages are being blessed in some societies, and there is strong agitation for churches to conduct same-sex marriages. Some Christian denominations allow homosexual and lesbian ministers in their pulpits. It is necessary to address this subject.

Those who are organizing support for homosexual and lesbian practices are twisting the word of God to suit their vile attitudes, and they harm their own consciences. The following passages from the Bible describe and strongly condemn unnatural unions. Only male and female bodies were created by God perfectly for each other.

> "Do not lie with a man as one lies with a woman; that is detestable. Do not have sexual relations with an animal and defile yourself with it, a woman should not present herself to an animal to have sex with it; that is a perversion" (Lev. 18: 22–23).

> "Do you not know that the wicked will not inherit the Kingdom of God? Do not be deceived, neither the sexually immoral nor idolaters nor adulterers nor male prostitutes nor homosexual offenders nor thieves nor the greedy nor drunkard nor slanderer nor swindlers will inherit the Kingdom of God" (1 Cor. 6: 9–10)

Beloved, these are the common sins of Sodom and Gomorrah which brought the wrath of God upon these cities for total destruction (Gen. 19: 4–25). To fully understand how homosexuality and lesbianism (sexual relations between members of the same sex) are sexual sins, one must first understand the eternal nature of our gender and how the powers of procreation are sacred. In the following section, learn more about same-sex attraction and how Satan would have us believe that homosexual and lesbian relations are not a sin.

Attraction between a man and woman was instilled by the Creator to ensure the perpetuation of life and to draw husband and wife together in the family setting that He prescribed for the accomplishment of His purposes, including the raising of children. Any deviation from God's commandments in the use of procreative powers is a grave sin. Therefore, homosexuality and lesbianism are wrong! This behaviour is unnatural; it is abnormal; it is an affliction of the devil. When practiced, it is immoral. It is a transgression and gross violation of God's commandment. Do not be misled by those who whisper that it is part of your nature and therefore right for you. That is false, and it is manipulation from the devil.

Homosexual and lesbian thoughts and feelings are a result of the devil's invasion and manipulation of the human mind and should be resisted, as our thoughts and feelings can lead us to undesired actions. Satan would have us believe that homosexual and lesbian relationships are not a sin, but they are, and they can lead a person into the destructive cycle of addiction. Breaking God's law of chastity through the sins of homosexual and lesbian activities causes a person to become spiritually dead.

Atheists loudly defend the rights of homosexuals and lesbians to pursue their lifestyles; however, this must be avoided by Christians. Furthermore, atheists promote the erroneous view that God is unfair and oppressive towards them. In reality, does God hate homosexuals and lesbians, or are His prohibitions a supreme manifestation of love and deep concern for His children?

God has made His commandments about homosexuality and lesbianism clear from the beginning. He declared in both the Old and the New Testament that homosexuality is a sin and that He strongly disapproves of its practices.

Some people erroneously assume that this disapproval manifests hatred on God's part toward His children who have chosen to practise homosexuality; in fact, this is far from the truth. His prohibitions really indicate a deep love for his children and an attempt to keep them from choices that can cause them serious harm, shorten their lives dramatically, and deny them access to the kingdom of God.

I would recommend deliverance for anyone who is practising homosexuality, lesbianism, or incest. By attending powerful deliverance services, people practising these lifestyles can obtain spiritual deliverance from these demonic afflictions, in the same way that those who are possessed by witchcraft and familiar spirits are delivered.

## The Fall of Satan

The Bible provides an account of the esteemed attributes and position of Lucifer, also known as Satan, the devil, or the serpent, when he resided in heaven and what caused his fall to the earth. It says, "You were anointed as a guardian cherub, for so I ordained you. You were on the holy mount of God; you walked among the fiery stones. You were blameless in your ways from the day you were created till wickedness was found in you" (Ezek. 28: 14–15).

God gave Satan a certain degree of power and authority in heaven as the head of choir, but he arrogantly perverted his position with the determination to exalt himself above God's throne when pride and greed entered him. The scripture records it thus: "All your pomp has been brought down to the grave, along with the noise of your harps; maggots are spread out beneath you and worms cover you. How you have fallen from heaven, O Lucifer, son of the morning star! You have been cast down to the earth, you who once laid low the nations! You said in your heart, 'I will ascend to heaven; I will raise my throne above the stars of God; I will sit enthroned on the mount of assembly, on the utmost heights of the sacred mountain. I will ascend above the tops of the clouds; I will make myself like the Most High.' Yet you shall be brought down to Sheol, to the lowest depths of the pit" (Isa. 14: 11–15 NIV).

The Bible also says "Pride comes before destruction, a haughty spirit before fall" (Prov. 16: 18 NIV). We could infer from this that pride leads to disobedience, and disobedience leads to death.

The following verses describe how Satan, the dragon, was hurled onto the earth from heaven and became the inhabitant of the garden of Eden, a wanderer without any designation whatsoever.

> You were in Eden, the garden of God; every precious stone adorned you: ruby, topaz and emerald, chrysolite, onyx and jasper, sapphire, turquoise and beryl. Your settings and mountings were made of gold; on the day you were created they were prepared. (Ez. 28: 13 NIV)

> The great dragon was hurled down, that ancient serpent called the devil or Satan, who deceives the whole world; he was hurled to the earth and his angels with him. (Rev. 12: 9 NIV)

The Bible records that after Satan fell to the earth, he was in the garden of Eden as a wanderer, pursuing his rebellious attitude, this time toward humankind, fighting to bring humankind down into the pit as a form of revenge against God. "Even persecution makes overcomers stronger. Those who stand for Christ and bear a strong testimony of the truth will surely face persecution and trials, but victory is assured for the faithful. The Bible says, "Then the dragon was enraged at the woman and went off to make war against the rest of her offspring those who obey God's commandments and hold to the testimony of Jesus" (Rev. 12: 17 NIV).

Beloved in Christ, don't be deceived. The devil is the number-one enemy of humans, with a strong, clear agenda to steal, to kill, and to destroy (John 10: 10). Having lost his place in heaven, all that was left for him was to implement his diabolical agenda against the children of God through wrestling and scuttling man's blessing. The Bible says: Be self-controlled and alert. Your enemy the devil prowls around like a roaring lion looking for someone to devour resist him, standing firm in the faith, because you know that your brothers throughout the world are undergoing the same kind of suffering" (1 Pet. 5: 8–9)

The serpent (the devil) studied and understood the relationship between the first couple; he was fully aware of the gap in their relationship and the vulnerable nature of the woman prior to his attack; he cleverly opened up the accusations thus: "Now the serpent was more crafty than any of the wild animals the Lord God had made. He said to the woman, did God really say, you must not eat from any tree in the garden?" Satan launched the attack to manipulate the woman's mind against the law of the Lord, and he is still doing the same thing today. Many people, like Adam and Eve, clearly understand the law of the Lord but are being manipulated by the devil to disobey God so that Satan can harm their soul through various devices like sex or lying. The Bible continues "The woman said to the serpent, we may eat fruit from the trees in the garden, But God did say, you must not eat fruit from the tree that is in the middle of the garden and you must not touch it or you will die" (Gen. 3: 1–3)

The serpent launched the attack and manipulated the woman during her lonely hours in order to get the man and woman to disobey God so he could plunge humankind into the pit and steal the glory God gave man: "You will not surely die, the serpent said to the woman. For God knows that when you eat of it your eyes will be opened, and you will be like God knowing good and evil" (Gen 3: 4–5).

Surely, the devil twisted the truth about the forbidden fruit to the woman and tempted her to eat it, leading to humankind's spiritual death. Disobedience has no other name. God gave his instruction: "And the Lord God commanded the man, you are free to eat from any tree in the Garden, but you must not eat from the tree of the knowledge of good and evil, for when you eat of it you will surely die" (Gen. 3: 16–17). However, the serpent gave the woman an alternative opinion to this commandment, and she ate the fruit. Here, sin was introduced into human history for the first time; Adam and Eve were confronted with the consequences of sin: suffering and death.

The devil offered the woman a choice to disobey God's commandment; he clouded the meaning of the commandment by distorting the consequences associated with the act of disobedience, saying, "You will not surely die." What a deception. Beloved, the devil will never repent of his deceptive, evil attack on man until his appointed time. Your adversary **the devil** as a roaring lion walks about **seeking whom** he may devour (1 Peter 5:8). The woman's choice ushered in suffering and distorted the institution of marriage, establishing a place for evil in the perfect world. The devil, the number-one enemy of our souls, succeeded in devouring the disobedient couple. From the time the first couple was expelled from the garden of Eden, every inclination of the thoughts of human hearts was always evil. The world today is chaotic and lacks peace.

## The Devil's Attack

The perfect world and perfect form of marriage instituted by God, which was meant to bring about peace, comfort, and blessing for mankind, was attacked and distorted through Satan's deception; he influenced human disobedience to God's commandment. This resulted in God's severance of relationship with man and brought judgement to Adam and Eve (spiritual death) for the sin of disobedience, and they were expelled from the garden of Eden.

No matter how much the devil tries to usurp authority from God, God's sovereign authority over His creation stands. He has not relegated His authority, and neither has He abdicated His throne; He delegated His authority to man, not to the devil. God's sovereign authority created and sustains the earth, and violating His rules automatically leads to greater suffering.

Many have invited curses into their family by a lack of understanding about the significance attached to marriage. Many men have abused and treated their wives as second class instead of seeing them as the flesh of their flesh and bone of their bones;

likewise, some women have mishandled and abused God's glory in their lives by kicking their husbands out of their homes.

Some people have fallen into the satanic trap of adultery, which is the only reason allowed by the law of Moses for dissolution of marriage, but have failed to consider the effects of adultery and divorce in the lives of family members and in the sight of God.

The world has become chaotic and full of evil due to the destruction of the foundational values of life, and this has clouded the glory of the marriage institution. However, unless you are born again, it may not be possible to know and meet the fullness of God's vision for marriage.

**Let your marriage be established as an altar where sacrifices of love, truth, forgiveness, holiness, and righteousness are laid daily to attract the presence of God and His blessings in your family.**

## Chapter Two

# EVIL AND SPIRITUAL BLINDNESS

### The Falling Man

Paradise became a courtroom, and the keepers of the garden, Adam and Eve, became criminals on trial. There are two parts to the judgement scene. Before God passed judgement, He called out to Adam and asked, "Where are you?" (Gen. 3: 9).

Husbands and wives, where are you with your marriages? God is not ignorant of where you are hiding in your marriage; He summons you to come out of your hiding spots. Don't hide your nakedness; He is aware of all your iniquities. Don't give any excuses; simply confess, repent, and ask for forgiveness from your God.

The Bible says: "Come now, let us reason together says the Lord. Though your sins are like scarlet, they shall be as white as snow, though they are red as crimson, they shall be like wool. If you're willing and obedient, you will eat the best from the land" (Isa. 1: 18–19).

**Self-conquest is the greatest conquest. A person who conquers others is strong, but one who conquers oneself is mighty. Conquer the sinner man inside of you, and be a winner on the outside.**

David did not hide from his sins; he confessed them wholeheartedly. God, who created us, knows our sins. He has detailed records of our activities on earth, including our intentions. Our God is forgiving. He will not despise our broken hearts. "Unto the woman He said, I will greatly multiply thy sorrow and thy conception; in sorrow thou shall bring forth children and thy desire shall be to thy husband, and he shall rule over you" (Gen. 3: 16). This verse suggests that before the first couple's disobedience, marriage was not intended to be like a master and slave but a mutual relationship, with each spouse playing a unique role in the marriage. Therefore, maltreatment of wives or husbands is a pest that must be destroyed and suppressed by every married person. "And unto Adam he said, Because thou hast hearkened unto the word of thy wife, and has eaten of the tree, of which I commanded thee, saying, Thou shall not eat of it: cursed is the ground for thy sake: in sorrow shall thou eat of it all the days of Thy life. In the sweat of thy face shalt thou eat bread. Till return unto the ground for out of it was thou taken: for dust thou art and unto dust shalt thou return" (Gen. 3: 16–19 KJV).

Beloved, what would have happened if Adam had confessed and asked for forgiveness like King David did later? "Have mercy on me O God, according to your unfailing love, according to your great compassion blot out my transgression, wash away all my iniquity and cleanse away all my sin." (Ps. 51: 1–2) God would have tampered justice with mercy for Adam, because "a broken and a contrite heart, God will not despise" (Ps. 51: 17b NIV).

Remember the thief at the right hand of Jesus Christ on the cross? He acknowledged all his atrocities and confessed them to Jesus in the final moments of his life, and he obtained forgiveness and eternal life. "One of the criminals who hung there hurled insults at him; 'Aren't you the Christ? Save yourself and us.' But the other criminal rebuked him. 'Don't you fear God,' he said, 'since you are under the same sentence? We are punished justly, for we are getting what our deeds deserve. But this man has done nothing wrong.' Then he said, 'Jesus, remember me when you come into your kingdom.' 'I tell you the truth, today you will be with me in paradise'" (Luke 23: 39–43). Human unfaithfulness that betrays the marriage bond is an abomination before God and an abuse of His love. It is the foundation of suffering and poverty. The escape route from this suffering is repentance and confession, followed by forgiveness and being cleansed with the blood of the Lamb of God.

## Evil and Suffering

It's clear that the first couple's disobedience of eating the forbidden fruit led to human expulsion from the Garden of Eden and brought suffering for humanity (Gen. 3: 17–19).

Consequently, those first disobedient acts have had devastating effects on humanity from that time until today; disobedience has harmed the peace of the world and brought untold hardship to the entire human race. Thank God for the grace of salvation for fallen humankind, through the offspring of the woman that was deceived to eat the forbidden fruit at the garden of Eden. Christ was mandated to crush the head of the serpent and set the human race free from captivity ... "And I will put enmity between you (Satan) and the woman, and between your offspring and hers; he will crush your head, and you will strike his heel" (Gen. 3: 15). God's love for man has no end. Another aspect of the escape route provided for man is the grace of God through the atoning blood of Jesus Christ who is "the offspring of the woman," (Genesis 3:15) which is more valuable than anything. The Bible says, "Then you shall know the truth and the truth will set you free" (John 8: 32).

## Freedom

Freedom starts from knowing the truth about God and why He created man in His image and after his likeness; it also includes knowing His plan for marriage and accepting the gift of His only begotten Son to die on the cross at Calvary for our redemption. The Bible says, "For God so loved the world that He gave His only begotten Son (Jesus) that whosoever believes in Him will not die but have an everlasting life" (John 3: 16).

God sacrificed His Lamb on the cross for our propitiation and set us free from the bondage of sin; this act broke the gates of prisons that held the sinners hostage, and Jesus sent the Holy Spirit to abide with us. Before His ascension to the cross, Jesus Christ said in the book of John that: "The thief comes only to steal and kill and to destroy. I have come that they (man) may have life and have it full" (John 10: 10).

God brought all prophesy to fulfilment in Jesus Christ, to lift fallen man out of the pit of darkness to light and from poverty to riches, slavery to freedom, and death to life. The Bible says, "But upon mount Zion there shall be deliverance, and there shall be holiness; and the house of Jacob shall possess their possession" (Ob. 1: 17).

Christ's death on the cross at Calvary and His resurrection brought freedom and enabled believers to possess what was stolen and destroyed by the devil.

## Fornication

The sexual act is more spiritual than it is physical; do not play with it. Sexual sin is the most powerful means by which the devil destroys anointing in the life of men and women of God. The devil sends out his beautiful women and handsome men as his agents to seduce men and women to have sexual intercourse and to cause havoc. Fornication is the act of sexual interaction between unmarried people. The Bible warns, "Flee fornication. Every sin that a man doeth is without the body but he that commiteth fornication sinned against his own body" (1 Cor. 6: 18 KJV).

Most singles engage in casual sexual relationships and call it fun, but it is an abomination before God. It is a channel by which venereal diseases, including HIV, are spread, destroying lives and causing barrenness. Fornication has destroyed many people's destinies and resulted in millions of unwanted pregnancies and abortions, the latter of which is murder. The Bible commands, Thou shall not commit murder and whoever commits murder faces judgement" (Matt. 5: 21 KJV).

Fornication and adultery are against the law of the Lord; unless people who practice these things repent, they will deprive themselves of their place in the kingdom of God (See 1 Cor. 6: 9–10; Gal. 5: 19–21, and Rev. 21: 8). God sternly warns against sexual perversion in Romans 1: 18–32; His message in Leviticus 18: 1–30 is also very clear and strong.

The unwanted pregnancies that come from fornication and adultery often lead people to having abortions, which is undoubtedly one of the most heinous sins that continues to be committed around the world. The sin of abortion is the gruesome murder and slaughter of innocent unborn babies in their mother's wombs in the name of unwanted pregnancy. Abortion involves the shedding of innocent blood. It violates the Golden Rule, destroys the work of God, annuls the plans of God, devalues human values and lacks natural affection.

To all Christian women out there who have had abortions in the past but have realized the seriousness of their mistake and have confessed this sin and asked for and received forgiveness from God, congratulations. To those who have not confessed and repented of this sin, please do so without hesitation. And to those who have not committed this heinous sin, please stay clear of it and don't attempt it. It is murder of innocent souls.

The church has a great responsibility to teach our children from the time they are an appropriate age in the children's ministry and the youth ministry to abstain from casual sex before they get married. This is a big challenge for the church and for Christian parents all over the world. Although the world has obscured the harm of fornication, but the word of God stands sure. It says, "But you are a chosen people, a royal priesthood, a holy nation, a people belonging to God, that you may declare the praises of him who call you out of darkness unto his wonderful light" (1 Pet. 2: 9).

## Adultery

God's commandment against adultery in the Bible is very strict: "Thou shall not commit adultery" (Exod. 20: 14). Adultery is an act of sexual immorality committed by a married person outside of their marriage bond. It is the only cogent reason allowed for the dissolution of marriage.

Adultery is an act of unfaithfulness that breaks the marriage bond. It abuses the honourable institution of marriage, established by God and intended as a one-flesh union, which the couple entered into in the presence of God and man. Through adultery, Satan steals the blessing and denies those who practise adultery a place in the kingdom of God. Once adultery sets into a family, hatred gives birth to bitterness. The Bible says, "Do you not know that the wicked will not inherit the Kingdom of God? Neither the sexually immoral nor idolaters nor adulterers nor male prostitutes nor homosexual offenders nor thieves nor the greedy nor drunkards nor slanderers nor swindlers will inherit the kingdom of God" (1 Cor. 6: 9–10).

Paul's epistle to the Galatians puts it this way: "Now the works of the flesh are manifest, which are these, *adultery, fornication,* uncleanness, lasciviousness, Idolatry, witchcraft, hatred, variance, emulations, wrath, strife, seditions, heresies, envying, murders, drunkenness, revelling, and such like: of the which I tell you before, as I have also told you in time past, that they which do such things shall not inherit the kingdom of God" (Gal. 5: 19–21, emphasis mine).

This is the truth: the devil has no permanent place of abode; he is a spirit without a living body, roaming about and taking over bodies that give him legal entrance through the points of entry, namely: the eyes to see, ears to hear, nose to smell, hands to touch, and mouth to taste. The devil will not seek permission to invade your body; all he does is to look for vulnerability through sins, such as those listed in the above scriptures. Satan invades people's lives like a thief in the night, in order to steal, kill, and to destroy people's lives and destinies. The Bible says, "Do you not know that your bodies are member of Christ Himself? Shall I then take the member of Christ and unite them with a prostitute? Never, do you not know that he who unites himself with a prostitute is one with her in body? For it is said, the two will become one flesh" (1 Cor. 6: 15–16).

When the devil afflicts a Christian home with adultery and fornication, the results are like what they were for Adam and Eve in the garden of Eden. These sins are a dangerous trap and legal grounds for the devil and his demons to enter human lives and cause havoc. The Bible warns, "Be self-control and alert, your enemy the devil prowl around like a roaring lion looking for someone to devour" (1 Pet. 5: 8).

Sexual union is God's plan to create physical and emotional unity in marriage relationships; it is supposed to be a sacred act between a husband and wife to bring about the manifestation of God's blessing. Paul reminds believers to "flee from sexual immorality. All other sins a man commits are outside his body, but he who sins sexually sins against his own body. Do you not know that your body is a temple of the Holy Spirit, who is in you, whom you have received from God? You are not your own; you were bought at a price. Therefore honour God with your body" (1 Cor. 6: 18–20).

## Abraham's Example

Abraham was an obedient servant of God. The Bible describes him as a faithful and righteous man. Abraham secured a covenant promise from God that he would become the father of a nation, but

Abraham had an extramarital sexual relationship with Hagar, the servant of his wife, Sarah. It was Sarah's suggestion for Abraham to do so in order for him to have an heir, but certainly it was against God's principle for a marriage of a one-flesh union. That choice was recorded as adultery. The extramarital relationship between Hagar and Abraham produced Ishmael, who eventually became the father of the most violent tribes in the world and robbed the world of peace. Foretelling this, an angel said, "And he will be a wild donkey of a man; his hand will be against everyone and everyone's hand will be against him and he will live in hostility toward all his brothers" (Gen. 16: 12 NIV).

This is the origin of hate, bitterness, and violence between the descendants of two rival children, Ishmael and Isaac, leading to many generations of terrorists in the world.

Adultery and fornication are the most cunning afflictions on humanity. Engaging in these sins spreads diseases, sicknesses, and untimely deaths to millions of people old and young, the world over. They have destroyed destinies and love within families, and they ignite hatred in couple's hearts, leading to bitterness and divorce. Adultery is both toxic and destructive to a family unit; when it enters into a family's life, its effects can only be stopped by the intervention of God.

## Abraham and Abimelech

When Abraham and his wife, Sarah, sojourned in the land of the Negev, in the village of Gerar. Because of the wickedness of the land, Abraham could not claim outright that he was Sarah's husband for fear of being assassinated. Abimelech, the king of Gerar, took Sarah, but God showed Abraham and his wife Sarah including King Abimelech and his people how important it is to avoid adultery.

> Now Abraham moved on from there into the region of the Negev and lived between Kadesh and Shur for a while he stayed in Gerar, and there Abraham said of his wife Sarah, she is my sister. Then Abimelech king of Gerar sent for Sarah and took her. But God came to Abimelech in a dream one night and said to him, "You are as good as dead because of the woman you have taken; she is married." (Gen. 20: 1–3)

This is the extent that God can show anger towards anyone who commits adultery. It carries grave consequences. Similar circumstances also occurred between Abraham and Pharaoh in Egypt (see Gen. 12: 14–20).

## Jacob's Example

Jacob found himself in polygamous family relationships; he had twelve sons born from four wives. Jacob's children – except Benjamin, the youngest, who had the same mother as Joseph – hated Joseph and conspired against him because of his dream. "His brothers said to him, do you intend to reign over us? Will you actually rule us? And they hated him all the more because of his dream and what he had said" (Gen. 37: 8).

Jacob's sons sold Joseph into slavery and, as a result, they effectively sold the entire household of Jacob into slavery. This wicked act eventually led to the enslavement of the children of Israel in Egypt for over 400 years as foretold to Abraham: "Then the Lord said to him, 'Know for certain that your descendants will be strangers in a country not their own, and they will be enslaved and mistreated for four hundred years. But I will punish the nation they serve as slaves, and afterward they will come out of it with great possessions'" (Gen. 15: 13–14). God's faithfulness to His word set the Israelites free from this captivity in Egypt through Moses.

People of God, sit back and ask yourself this question: what would have happened if all the children of Jacob had come from the same womb? Would they have hated Joseph all the more and sold him into slavery just the same? My answer is no. They would not have done this in the first place unless they were under the influence of evil, demonic powers or unless it was ordained by God for them to do so. My research on polygamous homes shows that bitterness, hatred, disunity, and lovelessness thrive in almost every polygamous home, as they did in Jacob's family.

Beloved, with the help of the Holy Spirit, you can break loose from the foundational errors of your generation and help others to follow suit. Whilst you do that, God's presence will fill you and build His fortress around you.

## David's Example

King David was an anointed man of God, but even his good relationship with God did not spare him from the cunning spirit of adultery.

King David had an adulterous spirit and lived a polygamous life. The devil entered his heart and caused him to covet Bathsheba, the wife of Uriah, one of the king's loyal servants. After this, David committed the sexual sin of adultery with Bathsheba and then manipulated the war to kill her husband and take Bathsheba as his wife.

Because of this evil act, the judgement of God was raised against King David through the prophet Nathan, who said, "Why did you despise the word of the Lord by doing what is evil in his eyes? You struck down Uriah the Hittite with the sword and took his wife to be your own. You killed him with the sword of the Ammonites. Now therefore, the sword will never depart from your house because you despise me and took the wife of Uriah to be your own" (2 Sam. 12: 9–10).

A string of sins always produces estrangement from God. The string of sins committed by David's sons Absalom and Amnon were no exception. They involved lust, deceit, rape, hatred, drunkenness, murder, and incest and were no exception. The consequences of the sin of adultery in David's life were devastating and horrible. His son Ammon fell in love with Tamar, daughter of David and sister to Absalom. The biblical account reads: "Then Amnon said to Tamar, bring the food here into my bedroom so I may eat from your hand. And Tamar took the bread she had prepared and brought it to her brother Amnon in his bedroom. But when she took it to him to eat, he grabbed her and said, 'come to bed with me, my sister.' 'Don't my brother,' she said to him. Don't force me. Such a thing should not be heard in Israel. Don't do this wicked thing. What about me? Where could I get rid of my disgrace? And what about you? You would be like one of the wicked fools in Israel. Please speak to the king; he will not keep me from being married to you.' But he refused to listen to her, and since he was stronger than she, he raped her. Then Amnon hated her with intense hatred. In fact, he hated her more than he had loved her" (2 Sam. 13: 10–14 NIV).

This was the beginning of the manifestation of the sword in the house of David. Bitterness and hatred thrived in David's household, which led to Absalom plotting against Ammon and eventually killing him. "Absalom ordered his men, 'listen! When Amnon is in high spirits from drinking wine and I say to you, "Strike Amnon down," then kill him. Don't be afraid. Have not I given you this order. Be strong and brave.' So, Absalom's men did to Amnon what Absalom had ordered. Then all the king's sons got up, mounted their mules and fled" (2 Sam. 13: 28–29 NIV).

Adultery is a gateway for eternal damnation; it invites negative consequences. It also leads to divorce and establishes the foundation of corruption that leads to the breakdown of the law and other values in society. It destroys family values and leads to crimes being committed by the youth in that society. It is the foundation for human problems and suffering. Absalom, the son of David, conspired and rebelled against his own father to enthrone himself as a king over Israel in place of his father. David and his official had to flee from Jerusalem to escape from Absalom. As there was estrangement in the house of David, so could there be in any family or church where adultery is freely practised.

Meditate on your present circumstances and let your conscience speak to you as you read this book. Is there any sin of adultery that you have yet to confess and repent? Please settle with God to secure peace and happiness in your marriage and family.

## Solomon's Example

King Solomon was a child of adultery himself; his birth brought the sword into the house of King David. King Solomon was also deeply involved in a polygamous system of marriages, as he had many wives and concubines. His foreign wives influenced Solomon to build altars for their foreign gods, which was considered idolatry in Israel. This was against God's commandment, and the land of Israel was defiled with idols. Solomon's actions provoked God's anger upon the nation of Israel because his loyalty to God was compromised through the worship of idols, by the influence of his adulterous life.

> The Lord became angry with Solomon because his heart has turned away from the Lord, the Lord of Israel, who had appeared to him twice. Although he had forbidden Solomon to follow other gods, Solomon did not keep the Lord's command. So the Lord said to Solomon, "Since this is your attitude and you have not kept my covenant and decrees which I commanded you, I will most certainly tear the kingdom away from you and give it to one of your subordinates. Nevertheless, for the sake of David your father, I will not do it during your lifetime. I will tear it out of the hand of your son. Yet I will not tear the whole kingdom from him but will give him one tribe for the sake of David my servant and for the sake of Jerusalem which I have chosen. (1 Kgs. 11: 9–13)

Solomon's polygamous marriages introduced false religions to Israel; God saw this as sin and visited the nation with His judgement as recorded in the scripture. In the day of King Rehoboam, the son of Solomon, God divided Israel, which had once been golden and glorious, into two nations: the northern kingdom of Israel and the southern kingdom of Judah.

When all Israel saw that the king refused to listen to them, they answered the king 'what share do we have in David' what part in Jesse's son? To your tents O Israel' Look after your own house O David. So the Israelites went home, but as for the Israelites who were living in the town of Judah, Rehoboam still ruled over them. (1 Kgs. 12: 16–17)

Have you ever sat down to ask why anyone who practises adultery and fornication will not enter the kingdom of God? Have you ever meditated on how the sin of adultery committed by individuals like Abraham, Jacob, King David, and Solomon could affect a nation and generations of humans? The answer is simple. Adultery and fornication pervert the perfect will of God and harm the initially perfect world of man; as mentioned previously, these sins distort marriages and families and produce bitterness and hatred. The Apostle Paul warned the Galatians and Ephesians with the following words: "Now the works of the flesh are manifest, which are these, adultery, fornication, uncleanness, idolatry, witchcraft, hatred, variance, emulation, wrath, strife, sedition, heresies, envying, murders, drunkenness, revelling and such and the like I warn you, as I did before, that those who live life like this will not inherit the kingdom of God" (Gal. 5: 19–21).

"But among you there must not be even a hint of sexual immorality, or of any kind of impurity, or of greed, because these are improper for God's holy people" (Eph. 5: 3). Adultery has a harmful spiral effect.

## The Power of Vows and Promises

Vows and promises made at the altar during a wedding or during love relationships are highly spiritual, powerful, and binding when sex is involved.

As a company CEO, I was personally involved in the drafting and signing of business agreements between my establishment, Yaolat Technologies Limited, and banks, federal and state government ministries, as well as other companies in Nigeria. Similarly, many nations of the world also involves in economic, education and military treaties between themselves. These agreements are signed with pens, on paper, and sealed with handshakes across tables and can be nullify by either party. In contrast, every vow and promise made to establish conjugal relationships involves our bodies, souls, and spirits and is consummated during sexual intercourse. Practitioners may pretend to have revoke such relationship, for sure, they are still binding in the soul and spiritually.

Every fornicator and adulterer has in most cases shredded and shared his or her body, soul, and spirit with agents of Satan: men and women who are dedicated to idols, members of the occult, or practicing witchcraft. During their various acts of sexual immorality, these people ultimately seal their vows and promises with their own blood during their casual sexual relationships.

Many have inherited some demonic spirits in their lives and have lost their spiritual virtue in the process. A disobedient person acting as a satanic agent will deposit an evil substance to destroy, steal, and kill his or her partner's destiny and blessing.

I am not just making a statement or fabricating a story; I am speaking from experience as a minister of God's deliverance. Immoral sex is one of the greatest weapons that Satan and his demons use to steal, destroy, and kill. It is often used to manipulate the mind to disobey God's commandments so that Satan can have legal ground to invade a family and cause havoc in people's lives. The Bible says, "Do you not know that your bodies are members of Christ himself? Shall I then take the member of Christ and unite them with prostitutes? Never!" (1 Cor. 6: 15 NIV).

Sexual union is God's plan to create physical and emotional unity in the marriage relationship. Such unity is the foundation of the family. Participating in such union outside of a marriage commitment, which is adultery, destroys family life and is a betrayal of our faith in Christ, to whose body we belong and to whom we are united as His bride. Apostle Paul says: "Do you not know that he who unites himself with a prostitute is one with her in body? For it is said, the two shall become one flesh. But he who unites himself with the Lord is one with him in spirit. Flee from sexual immorality. All other sins a man commits are outside his body, but he who sins sexually sins against his own body" (1 Cor. 6: 16–18).

Sexual activities outside of wedlock are dangerous; they could invite a spiritual virus into a family and destroy the family's destiny. But when sex is morally and spiritually practised by married couples, it demonstrates the commitment to the marriage vow and faithfulness to Christ, with whom we are united spiritually. The end result is blessings for the family and their descendants yet unborn.

Let me further explain. God the Father, the Son, and the Holy Spirit are one and forever united. God expects Christian families of husband, wife and children to be united from one generation to another; the family is the extension of the Trinity on earth. A united family is a witness of the Triune God. The existence of divided hearts amongst God's family members is not God's will. Therefore, God is forever looking for families that are united, dedicated, and loving in body, soul, and spirit to release His blessings to, as it was in the beginning in the garden of Eden.

## Divorce Is against the Will of God

The miraculous pregnancy and birth of our Lord Jesus Christ by the Virgin Mary, made possible through the Holy Spirit (Luke 1: 26–33), symbolises the rebirth of humanity, particularly for those who believe in the sonship, death, and resurrection of Jesus Christ (John 3: 16). It also signifies the re-enactment of the ordinances of God's love over all created order as in the beginning.

Let me therefore make the following significant insights into the spirituality of marriage and the peril of divorce.

In the beginning, man was formed from the dust of the ground and was lifeless until he received the breath of God, the Holy Spirit, to become a living soul. Man was made in the image and likeness of God and was qualified to be a representative of God, managing the fullness of the earth on God's behalf.

God made it His topmost priority to empower man for replenishing the earth and taking full dominion by providing a true helpmate for Adam and crowning the work of creation through instituting marriage. The Bible says, "It is not good for a man to be alone, I will make a helper suitable for him" (Gen. 2: 18).

God formed the first woman with the bone removed from Adam's rib and presented her to Adam as a wife, then, God commanded oneness of flesh and bone between a man and a woman in marriage as an everlasting ordinance (see Gen. 2: 24).

The rib is a protective organ; it covers sensitive organs like the lungs, liver, kidney, and heart. This denotes that wives are to be protected, loved, and cared for in marriage.

Similar to God breathing into man at creation, the Holy Spirit came upon Mary, and the power of the Most High God overshadowed her, and the Holy One was conceived and born of her. In the same manner, the church was drawn out from the rib of our Lord Jesus Christ through His atoning blood on the cross and His death and resurrection. The Bible says, "Husbands, love your wives, just as Christ loved the Church and gave himself up for her, to make her holy, cleansing her by the washing with water through the word, and to present her to himself as a radiant Church without stain or wrinkle or any other blemish, but holy and blameless. In this same way, husbands ought to love their wives as their own bodies. He who loves his wife loves himself" (Eph. 5: 25–28). The above bible passage confirmed the divinity and sacredness of marriage acts to be guided jealously by husbands and wives. Then, I heard what sounded like a great multitude, like the roar of rushing waters and like loud peals of thunder shouting: Hallelujah! For our Lord God Almighty reigns. Let us rejoice and be glad and give him glory!

For the wedding of the Lamb has come and his bride 'Church' has made herself ready. Fine linen, bright and clean, was given her to wear. (Fine linen stands for the righteous acts of the saints" (Rev. 19: 6–8). This symbolises the ideal Godly or Christian marriage that must be kept till the end.

The foundation of marriage that was laid out by our ancestors has a lot of influence on our own lives. Divorce is a wrong foundation in this area. The Bible says: "'I hate divorce' says the Lord God of Israel, 'and I hate a man covering himself with violence as well as with his garment' says the Lord Almighty. So guide yourself in your spirit and do not break faith" (Mal. 2: 16). Divorce is annulment of marriage, a reversal of wedding vows, and a rejection of God's will. The rate of divorce among Christian and non-Christian couple nowadays, including clergy of different denominations, is increasing at an alarming rate; many do not understand why they cannot cope with their marriage and therefore opt for divorce. Some couples who are not divorced only manage to live together as co-tenants, but communication has already broken down completely. They are enduring their marriage instead of enjoying it. If, therefore, our ancestors had faulty marriage relationships, we need to return to God to break the foundational problems in our marriages.

A young man named Alex, age 19, fell in love with his choice of a beautiful young lady who was 18. They remained faithful to each other and were deeply in love throughout their days in the university as they both attained first and second degrees and secured lucrative jobs in reputable organisations. Their parents supported their marriage and spent lavishly for their wedding. They had a good marriage, bought their first property, and were blessed with two kids. Unfortunately, misunderstandings arose between them, and they were later divorced. Why would this happen after they spent their youth and blessed married years together? Similar incidents have happened between millions of couples around the world; in fact, a large percentage of married couples in Europe and America have experienced divorce. Many couples have called it quits in less than one year of marriage. Speaking of curses for disobedience, the Bible says "You will be pledged to be married to a woman, but another will take her and ravish her. You will build a house, but you will not live in it. You will plant a vineyard, but you will not even begin to enjoy its fruit" (Deut. 28: 30).

Have you ever wondered why this is a common scenario among couples all over the world, particularly in developed and industrialised nations where God's authority is no longer respected? Have you ever wondered why your marriage, in which you enjoyed tremendous love and affection in the past, suddenly went sour? To answer this, first evaluate the level of disobedience to God in your relationship that could have given the devil ground to invade your marriage. The Bible says, "However, if you do not obey the Lord your God and do not carefully follow all his commands and decrees I am giving you today, all these curses will come upon you and overtake you." (Deut. 28: 15). The explanation of these types of situations is predicated on the fact that every Christian is required to obey the Lord and carefully keep all his commands. If we do so, we will receive blessings on our land, children, and possessions, but if we do not, we will receive curses for disobedience whatever we do and wherever we go.

Furthermore, as recorded in scripture, the curses are frightening. The scripture also says that because of the curses of disobedience, "Even the most gently and sensitive man among you will have

43

no compassion on his own brother or the wife he loves or his surviving children" (Deut. 28: 54) and "The most gentle and sensitive woman among you so sensitive and gentle that she would not venture to touch the ground with the sole of her foot will begrudge the husband she loves and her own son and daughter" (Deut. 28: 56). Seen in the context of divorce arising from the hardening of hearts, the scripture illustrates that disobedience to God is an underlying cause of divorce.

The truth remains that however deceptive, crafty, and manipulative the devil can be, God's words remain the supreme rules of life, and God has spoken loud and clear. Divorce is against the will of God, and disobedience to God's rules for life will continue to hurt the world. To this effect, the Bible says, "They eat the bread of wickedness and drink the wine of violence" (Prov. 4: 17).

The message of God concerning marriage is very clear. No one builds a house and wants it destroyed; God has built homes for His children, but the devil is working hard to destroy homes with violence, fornication, and adultery.

## Divorce Rates in the United Kingdom

According to the Office of National Statistics, divorce rates in the United Kingdom have risen again over the past few years after falling from the highest level, reached in 1996. The total number of divorces in England and Wales in 2004 was 153,490, which works out to 13.9 divorces per 1,000 married people. This rose from 13.4 in 2002.

## Number of Divorces in UK from 1938 to 1999

There were 160,000 divorces in England and Wales in 2002, an increase of almost 2 per cent from the 2001 figure of 157,000. Among these divorces, seven out of ten were the first divorce, so 70 per cent of divorces in the United Kingdom are the first divorce, and the average age at which couples split in the United Kingdom is 42 for men and 39 for women. Half of the couples who divorced have at least one child under 16 years of age.

Britain has the highest divorce rate and largest proportion of single parents in Europe, according to a Broken Hearts report. Figures show that a couple's prospects of a lasting marriage are bleaker in Britain than in any European Union country. Britain has 2.7 divorces per 1,000 of the population, compared with a European average of 1.8 between 1938 and 1999, according to Government figures in the study. Italy had the lowest rate at 0.6 divorces, while Spain registered 0.9, France 2.0, Austria 2.2, Germany 2.3, and Finland alongside Britain at 2.7. The high divorce rate, combined with the growth of cohabitation and illegitimate births, resulted in Britain recording the highest proportion of children living in one-parent families. More than a quarter of children in Britain now live in single-parent families, compared with a European average of 14 per cent. It is 6 per cent in Greece, 12 in Austria, 13 in France, 14 in Germany, and almost 15 per cent in Belgium.

In 2011 the number of divorces in England and Wales decreased by 1.7 per cent to 117,558, compared with 119,589 in 2010. This continues the general decline in divorces since 2003, when there were 153,065. The fall in divorces is consistent with a decline in the number of marriages up to 2009. The decrease in marriages during this time may be a result of the increasing number of couples choosing to cohabit rather than enter into marriage. See the following figure for a representation of this information.

**Figure 2: Number of marriages and divorces between 1931 and 2011 in England and Wales**

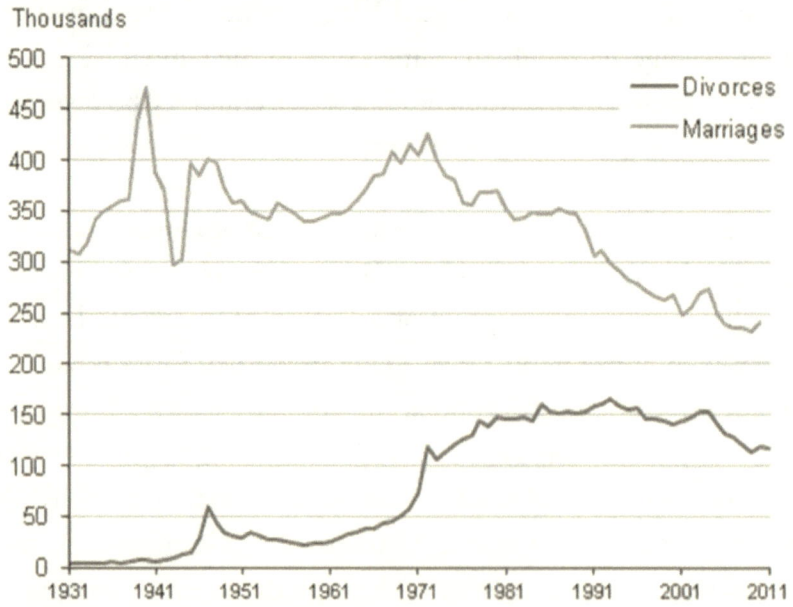

Source: Office for National Statistics

## Current Divorce Rate in America

It is frequently reported that the divorce rate in America is 50 per cent. Some schools of thought have said that this data is not accurate; however, it is reasonably close. The Americans for Divorce Reform organisation estimates that "Probably, 40 or possibly even 50 percent of marriages will end in divorce if current trends continue." This is a projection rather than statistics. The Bible says, "This know also, that in the last days perilous times shall come. For men shall be lovers of themselves, covetous, boaster, proud, blasphemers, disobedient to parents, unthankful, unholy" (2 Tim. 3: 1–2).

## Comparison of Recorded Marriage Ages for Those Who Divorce in America

| Age | Women | Men |
|---|---|---|
| Under 20 years old | 27.6% | 11.7% |
| 20 to 24 years old | 36.6% | 38.8% |
| 25 to 29 years old | 16.4% | 22.3% |
| 30 to 34 years old | 8.5% | 11.6% |
| 35 to 39 years old | 5.1% | 6.5% |

In America, 50 per cent of first marriages, 67 per cent of second, and 74 per cent of third marriages end in divorce, according to Jennifer Baker of the Forest Institute of Professional Psychology in Springfield, Missouri." However, a journal article on the divorce rate in America, in slight contrast to the above information, states that the divorce rate in America for a first marriage is 41 per cent, 60 per cent for second marriages, and 73 per cent for third marriages; but couples with children have a slightly lower rate of divorce than childless couples.

## International Rates of Divorce

| 1. | United States | 4.95 per 1000 people |
|---|---|---|
| 2. | Puerto Rico | 4.47 per 1000 people |
| 3. | Russia | 3.36 per 1000 people |
| 4. | United Kingdom | 3.08 per 1000 people |
| 5. | Denmark | 2.81 per 1000 people |
| 6. | New Zealand | 2.63 per 1000 people |
| 7. | Australia | 2.52 per 1000 people |
| 8. | Canada | 2.46 per 1000 people |
| 9. | Finland | 1.85 per 1000 people |
| 10. | Barbados | 1.21 per 1000 people |
| 11. | Qatar | 0.97 per 1000 people |
| 12. | Portugal | 0.88 per 1000 people |
| 13. | Tunisia | 0.82 per 1000 people |
| 14. | China | 0.79 per 1000 people |
| 15. | Singapore | 0.8 per 1000 people |
| 16. | Greece | 0.76 per 1000 people |
| 17. | Syria | 0.65 per 1000 people |
| 18. | Thailand | 0.58 per 1000 people |
| 19. | Mauritius | 0.47 per 1000 people |
| 20. | Ecuador | 0.42 per 1000 people |
| 21. | El-Salvador | 0.41 per 1000 people |
| 22. | Cyprus | 0.39 per 1000 people |
| 23. | Chile | 0.38 per 1000 people |
| 24. | Jamaica | 0.38 per 1000 people |
| 25. | Turkey | 0.37 per 1000 people |
| 26. | Mexico | 0.33 per 1000 people |
| 27. | Italy | 0.27 per 1000 people |
| 28. | Brazil | 0.26 per 1000 people |

The rate of divorce in African nations cannot be established as specifically from existing statistics, but my research shows that divorce in some African nations is very low, in part because of reasons explained in this book.

The dissolution of a marriage has a very devastating effect on the lives of family members concerned. The first impact of this ungodly process is the presence of the Holy Spirit disappearing from the lives of family members because of the bitterness and hate in their hearts. As Satan takes pre-eminence in the household, the husband is likely to become disorganised, confused, and irresponsible; his spiritual well-being is utterly destroyed. The woman is automatically stripped of the spiritual fortress built around her and is likely to be subjected to all sorts of insults and embarrassment. The children, the seed of the marriage, are worst hit. They become demoralised and lose the intimate affection of a home with united parents. This often deprives them of their positive sense of direction. Most children from broken homes often lead lives that are full of hostility and immoralities such as using drugs, stealing, fornicating, truancy, smoking, alcoholism, committing crimes and so forth. Such children constitute a terrible menace to their society.

Most of us know people who have gone through divorce; at best, it can be described as painful and perilous. The original marriage relationship is a real one, even when it has become distorted and destructive. Losing a husband or a wife is like losing a limb; it is a profound and violent trauma that may take years to heal or may never heal.

Jesus comments on the matter of divorce. What He says in Mark 10: 2–10 would seem to make divorce impossible, but Matthew's account allows infidelity as grounds for divorce (Matt. 19: 3–9).

> And the Pharisees came to him, and asked him, is it lawful for a man to put away his wife? Tempting him. And Jesus answered and said unto them. What did Moses command you? And they said, Moses suffered to write a bill of divorcement, and to put her away. And Jesus answered and said unto them, for the hardness of your heart he wrote you this precept. But from the beginning of the creation God made them male and female. For this cause shall a man leave his father and mother, and cleave to his wife, and they twain shall be one flesh; so then they are no more twain, but one flesh. What therefore God hath joined together, let not man put asunder. (Mark 10: 2–10)

After 1946, the Episcopal Church permitted the remarriage of a divorced person but only when a Bishop pronounced the judgement that no true Christian marriage had existed in the first place. While this canonical provision was moderately serviceable, it put the emphasis on a legalistic rather than pastoral approach to divorce. It also put the emphasis not on divorce but on remarriage. This provision rested on the curious and rather dubious theological proposition that a true Christian marriage is indissoluble, whereas another, presumably more ordinary, marriage may be dissolved. The anomaly caused by this contradiction finally led to the 1973 convention to adopt a new canon which explicitly recognised the termination of a marriage and the right of the partners to be remarried with the blessing of the church.

How can that decision be reconciled with the traditional Godly or Christian commitment to the permanence of the marriage bond? Many have raised this question and accused the church of abandoning traditional moral standards in an era that has no idea of what the church means by Christian marriage.

My research on marriage and family life shows that adult children of divorced parents lack a healthy "couple template", or model of marital partnership. By contrast, children from intact marriages generally take strength and encouragement from their parents' decision to stay together and their demonstration of the Christian principles of love, trustworthiness, perseverance, and endurance.

Many positive experiences common to children from intact families are not always visible in the life of children from broken homes. Adolescence tends to last longer for children of divorcees, because breaking free of their parents is more complicated than for their peers raised in intact families. To a striking extent, divorce is often a stumbling block to higher education.

Western civilisation and social-welfare support for single parents has made the institution of marriage a worse case than single parenthood, giving the woman power to kick her husband out of the house on the grounds of domestic violence. Some women have capitalised on the financial benefit that single parents can access in order to cause trouble for their husbands; some even use the police to chase their husbands out of the house. Doing this is evil; it is an invitation to curses. The scripture says that once a husband and wife are joined together and united as one; let no one split apart what God has joined together, they are no more twain but one (see Matt. 19: 6). The bible also says, "If you fully obey the Lord your God and carefully follow all his commands I give you today, the Lord your God will set you high above all the nations on earth. All these blessings will come upon you and accompany you if you obey the Lord your God" (Deut. 28: 1–2 NIV).

The marriage institution is God's sovereign idea for humans, whom He created in His image and likeness. Marriage cannot be conducted with human ideas or knowledge alone. The fear of God, love, truth, forgiveness, and absolute trust in God are the basic character qualities needed by the two individuals in the marriage bond to defeat the scheme of the devil. Divorce is a curse. It is not a solution to a family problem; it is just the beginning of suffering. It has ruined many lives and destroyed many destinies, and it should be avoided.

> And these words which I command thee this day shall be in thine heart. And thou shalt teach them diligently unto thy children, and shalt talk of them when thou sittest in thine house, and when thou walkest by the way, and when thou liest down, and when thou risest up. And thou shall bind them for a sign upon thine hand, and they shall be as fronlets between thine eyes. And thou shall write them upon the posts of thy house, and on thy gates. (Deut. 5: 6–9 KJV)

My research as a pastor and evangelist through the reading of much literature and having personal interactions with many men and women confirms that marriages in Asian and African countries are more stable, with lower divorce rates and a higher degree of respect for traditional moral values, than in the Western world. However, there is more repression of women in these regions than in the West. I did not extend my research to the Middle East because states in that region are predominantly Muslim.

Conservatives in the West are fond of saying that the traditional family is the bedrock of society. That view is held even more widely in Asia and Africa, where they viewed that the family is the focus of ethics and that a basic moral principle, self-improvement, can be pursued only within the confines of the family. This view agrees with what God says: it is not good for a man to be alone (Gen. 2: 18).

There are several distinct family systems in different regions of Asia. In South Asia, it is traditional to have arranged, early marriages, in which men are dominant and the extended family is important. East Asia also has a male-dominated system but one that stresses the nuclear family; nowadays, the culture there has abandoned arranged marriages. In South East Asia, women have somewhat more autonomy. But all three systems have escaped many of the social changes that have buffeted family life in the West since the 1960s.

In South Asia and China, marriage remains near universal, with 98 per cent of men and women tying the knot. In contrast, in some Western countries, a quarter of people in their thirties are cohabiting or have never been married, while half of new marriages end in divorce. Marriage continues to be the almost universal setting for childbearing in Asia: only about 2 per cent of births took place outside wedlock in Japan in 2007. Contrast that with Europe: in Sweden in 2008, 55 per cent of births were to unmarried women, while in Iceland the rate was 66 per cent.

Most East and South East Asian countries report little or no cohabitation. The exception is Japan, where, among women born in the 1970s, about 20 per cent say they have cohabited with a sexual partner. For Japan, that is a big change. In surveys conducted between 1987 and 2002, just 1 to 7 per cent of single women said they had lived with a partner. But it is not much compared with America where, according to a 2002 Gallup poll, over half of married Americans between the ages of 18 and 49 lived together before their wedding day. In many Western societies, more frequent cohabitation has offset a trend towards later marriage or higher rates of divorce. This has not happened in Asia.

Traditional attitudes live on in other ways. Compared with those in the West, Asians are more likely to agree with the statement that "happiness lies in marriage". They are also more likely to say women should give up work when they get married or have children and more likely to disapprove of premarital sex.

In my research, the reason there is such a low divorce rate in many parts of Africa today can be explained by the following factors.

1. Family ties. An African man lives for his people – family and friends – not just for himself.

2. Due to the extended family system, friends and family can always come in and chastise any of the married couples about their bad behavior. And the couple will listen.

3. Because almost everybody knows each other's wife or husband, there is less of a tendency to go out and cheat with a married person.

4. Women are generally of the view that leaving a man because he cheated on them is a waste of time because of a perception that the next one will cheat too. So, they stay, and with the help of family and friends, the issue is resolved.

5. On average, the African woman is conditioned by society to believe that if she treats her man right, he can have a fling, and he will surely come back home to her.

6. The chances of a woman who has given birth to a child getting married to a man without a child are very low in the African community. As a result, the woman is compelled to stay with her husband and make it work.

7. Very few African women try to control their household or their husband, no matter how much money they make compared to their husband. And those who have succeeded in getting a divorce because they are making more money than their husbands find it difficult to remarry, since the community sees these women as bossy.

8. Because some African societies still support polygamy, a woman is not quick to leave her man when he looks at other women, as long as he doesn't bring her home.

9. African men are encouraged by their family and friends to cheat but are quick to force the woman in a relationship to stay even when her husband cheats. It's a double standard, but that's the truth. The women cheat less than the men in this culture.

10. Western countries have a culture of me, me, me. When things go wrong in a marriage, the only person that counts is me, while an African woman would typically think about her children's future as a reason to stay in their marriage. As a whole, African women understand and respect the concept of a covenant marriage.

## Evaluating Marital Dissolution and Single Life in Old Age

One of the central themes of this book is the word of God which says, "It is not good for a man to be alone." (Gen. 2: 18). To provide a fuller perspective in consideration of this, I took time to speak with some people in Africa and Europe who ranged in age from 50 to 80 years old who have divorced and are living a single life in their old age with the view to establishing the challenges and values in lonely life? I gathered the following information.

I found out that very few women in this age group succeed in forming successful second or third marriages, while most divorced women between the ages of 40 to 60 years and above who are single parents have difficulties forming a steady marriage or relationship. The majority learn to cope with casual relationships or none, while some of them suffer some degree of loneliness, with the absence of an intimate relationship or love life, and end up developing depression and mental sickness.

These individuals may end up losing the affection of an intimate relationship for the rest of their lives. They end up relying on a carer who comes around to perform their daily responsibilities.

Men can easily form second, third or fourth marriages if they so desire, while most women find it extremely difficult to form second or third marriages once they have many children. However, most men are afraid to form second or third marriages for fear of the unknown. similarly, some women who have gone through the experience of divorce may not have absolute confidence or trust their new partner for anything but prefer casual relationship or partnership.

These are some of the reasons why the concept of Godly or Christian marriage and family life should be adhered to by every married couple, so they can enjoy a marriage with quality family values.

# Chapter Three

# THE NATURE OF GOD IN MARRIAGE

## The Love of God

Despite our shortcomings, the love of God for humankind remains the same throughout eternity. The Bible describes the foundation of God's love thus: "let us create man in our image in our likeness, and let them rule."

As mentioned previously in this book, God's love has no end and cannot be comprehended by human wisdom. The Bible also says, "For God so loved the world that He gave His only begotten Son that whosoever believes in him will not die but have everlasting love" John 3: 16.

God's love is incomparable. He created the fullness of the earth and conceived and created man in His likeness and gave the rulership of the earth to man. Beloved, as you read this book, take a deep breath and consider His love for you and me. Humankind disobeyed and rebelled against our Creator, yet He gave His only begotten Son, who offered Himself as a living sacrifice on the cross at Calvary to redeem us. Then He gave the Golden Rule (see Matt. 22: 37–40).

## Nature of Love

God is love; love does not originate in the world but from God. Love is the true nature of God, and for whoever does not love, the Bible says such a person does not know God.

> Dear friends, let us love one another, for love comes from God. Everyone who loves has been born of God and knows God. Whoever does not love does not know God, because God is love. (1 John 4: 7–8)

Love is the expression of the mind in thoughts, words, and action towards God and human beings to bring about joy, happiness, and blessings in our lives. Love flows from the heart of God the Father, the Son, and the Holy Spirit to the heart of man to be expressed to all humanity. If you claim to be a Christian and cannot love and forgive your spouse, it will be difficult for others to believe that you are a true Christian.

## Loving in Words

With the words "I love you", though they are short, a man and woman come together to establish God's counsel on earth. These words are so powerful that when they penetrate the hearts of a man and woman, they produce fuel to ignite the emotions that release submission and willingness for a one-flesh union.

Unfortunately, these soothing words are often forgotten by most husbands and wives after the ecstasy of their weddings. Why? This happens due to the devil's manipulation of the human mind. Words are so powerful. Saying the words "I love you", "honey", and "sweetheart" spices up the marriage, just as it is necessary for rain to fall frequently so that farmers reap a bountiful harvest. Likewise, it is important for couples to say "I love you" to each other every day. The relationship began with the use of these three words, and they should be used in thoughts, words, and actions to nurture the growth of marriage continuously.

The Bible points out the importance of voicing what one believes: "For with the heart man believeth unto righteousness and with the mouth confession is made unto salvation" (Rom. 10: 10).

## Love in Thoughts

Love begins when an essential matter of the heart finds expression through the mouth and actions. Husbands are to express the thoughts in their hearts to their wives and likewise wives to their husbands. The Bible says, "You brood of vipers, how can you who are evil say anything good? For out of the overflow of the heart the mouth speaks" (Matt. 12: 34).

Therefore, if a man's heart is filled with love, it finds expression in the words he speaks. If a man uses either abusive or respectful words for his wife, he is speaking out of the abundance of his heart. God expects men to be like Him and initiate love towards their wives; when a woman receives love, she will process and feel its presence. Husband, ignite the fuel of love between you and your wife. Surely, she will respond to it; no woman hates to be loved except anyone under the influence of familiar spirits. The Bible says, "Husbands, love your wives, just as Christ loved the Church and gave himself up for her" (Eph. 5: 25).

Love is a contagious and irresistible force; loving couples produce thriving fathers and mothers of future upright generations to build righteous nations. Love attracts peace and produces the seedbed for blessing, prosperity, and longevity. A well-known passage about love from the Bible says, "Love is patient, love is kind. It does not envy, it does not boast, it is not proud. It is not rude, it is not self-seeking, it is not easily angered, it keeps no record of wrongs. Love does not delight in evil but rejoices with the truth. It always protects, always trusts, always hopes, always perseveres. Love never fails" (1 Cor. 13: 4–8).

Wife, if you noticed a diminishing love from your husband, check your character to see whether or not it measures up to that of virtuous woman. If not, please adjust it, but if it does, then go on your knees to seek the face of the Lord (do not consult witch doctors or mediums). Keep your home smelling pleasant, the dining table filled with delicacies, and your bed fresh as you wear a welcoming smile.

## The Acts of Godly and Christian Marriage

God's desire for the institution of marriage is evident from the biblical account of creation (see Gen. 2: 18, 20–24).

Therefore shall a man leave his father and mother and cleave unto his wife and they shall be one fresh. Therefore they are not more twain but one flesh, what therefore God has joined together let no man put asunder. (Matt. 19: 4–9)

Marriage is a universal human institution which exists in every society. Can we then speak in any meaningful sense of "Christian marriage" if we mean that the Christian community should maintain a particular view of Godly or Christian marriage as laid out by God, even though it may also be shared by many outside the Christian community? Yes.

A Godly or Christian is a unique pattern for marriage because it is an honourable estate established and ruled by God's principles. Every married Christian couple must allow God to shepherd their marriage and allow the affairs in their lives to be controlled by God's will.

Marriage is an institution that was created by God for His Glory, and every rule governing the institution was duly established by God Himself. Therefore, couples are to be faithful to the fundamental bond of marriage.

In the past ages, the husband dominated the marriage; the wife was perceived to be his property, and no outside agencies could interfere with a husband's treatment of his wife. She could not own property. Women were often treated as slaves in the early marriage traditions. In many countries, the wife still has no independent legal rights; she is simply a housewife.

Although the early church acknowledged that marriage was ordained by God, many believed that marriage is only meant for procreation of children and for the perpetuation of humankind. However, God's intention for marriage was to provide a perfect companion and helpmate for the work of dominion. The Apostle Paul says, "It is better to marry than to be aflame with compassionate" (1 Cor. 7: 9). Marriage serves as a solution for concupiscence; that is, a legitimate context for accommodating sexual needs.

Most of us today find these older views of marriage unwelcome, if not revolting. It is clear that our view of Godly or Christian marriage has undergone some changes. Some of our presumptions have changed, while others have remained the same through the ages. These presumptions are summed up in the declaration of intention which is to be signed by anyone who seeks to be married in some of the orthodox church. This includes the following statement.

> We hold marriage to be a lifelong union of husband and wife. We believe it is for the purpose of mutual fellowship, encouragement, understanding, for the procreation (if it may be) of children and their physical and spiritual nurture and for safeguarding and benefit of society.

The Christian presumption is that marriage is intended to be permanent. This view is an outgrowth of the Biblical teaching that, in marriage, the man and woman become one flesh. Paul comments that if anyone joins his or her body to a harlot, the two become one flesh: "Do you not know that he who unites himself with a prostitute is one with her in body? For it is said the two will become one flesh" (1 Cor. 6: 16). Thus, sexual union creates and strengthens a deep and lasting bond between a couple, and especially between a husband and wife. It symbolises and celebrates that bond at the same time.

Marriage is the public expression by which a man and woman declare their intention to create and preserve such a bond by committing themselves to one another in a permanent, unconditional and unreserved union for better or for worse. They create a climate of security and stability within which sexual interaction can take place.

Since we are at our most vulnerable in times of intimacy, there is the potential to get hurt and fail in our sexual interactions. The security of permanence is necessary to enable full blooming of the deepest kind of intimate sexual relationship. Thus, the Christian community declares itself opposed to any casual contract of convenience, which is what most people in secular society practise and regard their marriages to be.

### Marriage Principles and Mutuality

Early Christians recognised that having an intimate relationship is one of the most significant aspects of marriage. The earliest prayer books listed mutual society as one of the purposes of marriage. Even the ancient writers of the Bible recognised that marriage helps overcome the loneliness of single life.

This view is in conformity with God's feelings expressed in Genesis 2: 18: "It is not good that man should be alone". Marriage can thus be seen as a testimony to the inherent social character of our humanity – we all need deep and lasting human companionship where intimate and caring relationship can flourish.

The conviction that the relationship of husband and wife should be founded on mutuality is a rather late development in Christian history. Paul's dictum was that the husband is the head of the wife "For the husband is the head of the wife as Christ is the head of the Church His body of which He is the Saviour" (Eph. 5: 23). This idea had long been accepted but was not interpreted in the sense of master and slave. Not until recently has this standard been challenged and ultimately repudiated. The marriage rite itself signalled the change when the 1928 Book of Common Prayer eliminated the traditional promise of the wife to love, honour, and obey her husband. Mutual vows were substituted, and thereafter, both husband and wife vowed to love, honour, and cherish each other.

Mutuality is more than theory; it sets a standard for equal treatment in the marriage, respect and honour for each other, and a common view on how to run the home. Not surprisingly, some men have found it hard not to expect their wife to wait on them, pick up their socks, cater to their whims, and make them the centre of their lives. In some parts of the world, even wives who work full-time are expected to do all the housework and the cooking. Many men still seem to feel demeaned if called upon to do housework.

Having a mutual relationship in marriage makes it appropriate for men to participate in domestic work. Of course, some division of labour is necessary in every marriage grounded in mutuality, where decisions are made together; neither partner is automatically required to perform any particular task or automatically excluded. Making decisions about housework is not easy, particularly when you consider the extra natural responsibilities of motherhood, such as carrying pregnancies to term, breast feeding, and caring for children. Now that women have entered the job market more extensively in most parts of the world, we can expect to see some changes in balancing work, life, and family obligations. When either the husband or wife is offered a new job or a promotion that requires a transfer, it often brings stress to the family and the marriage. In the past, the expectation was that a man's job was to take precedence, and the wife made the adjustments. Mutuality, however, demands that any such decision be faced and made together, not by one party acting alone.

## Jesus Redeemed Marriage.

As redeemer of the world, Jesus knew the perils of man. He had a deep knowledge and concern for the foundational values of life that had been destroyed. He knew where to begin the work of redemption; accordingly, Jesus started his ministry by providing for divine restitution of marriage at a wedding in Cana of Galilee. "Jesus said unto them, fill the water-pot with water. And they filled them up to the brim" (John 3: 7). Because Jesus was God incarnate on earth and had made the fullness of the earth (John 1: 1–3), He had full knowledge of God's intention for marriage. He also had full knowledge of how the devil had destabilised the first marriage to bring bitterness, sorrow, and suffering into human existence. Actually, Jesus' purpose on earth was to restore all that the devil had destroyed. Jesus declared, "My food is to do the will of He who sent me and to finish his work" (John 4: 34).

Jesus Christ removed bitterness from the institution of marriage and restored the sweetness that was meant for it from the inception of the world at the garden of Eden. When Jesus was done with the miracle at the wedding, He directed, "now draw some out and take it to the master of the banquet.

"And the master of the banquet tasted the water that had been turned into wine; he did not realise where it had come from, though the servant who had drawn the water knew. Then he called the bridegroom aside and said: everyone bring out the choice wine first and then the cheapest one after the guests have had too much to drink but you have saved the best till now" (John 2: 8–10).

Beloved, today's wars, hunger, suffering, and gnashing of teeth are the result of a distorted marriage institution. The ideal Godly or Christian marriage established by God was not meant to be the way we often see it. Jesus, the Messiah, took it as His primary responsibility to redeem and bless the marriage institution, which is the foundation of blessed life, during His ministerial activities on earth.

Our Lord Jesus Christ very emphatically told the Pharisees who were rigidly applying the law of Moses but blind to the grace of God, "Moses permitted you to divorce your wives because your hearts were hard but was not this way from the beginning. I tell you that anyone who divorces his wife except for marital unfaithfulness and marries another woman commits adultery" (Matt. 19: 8).

A Godly or Christian marriage bond demands that we don't attempt to change our spouse as we would change outfits or shoes. According to God's vision, marriage is supposed to be a lifetime school where the two partners involved in a one-flesh union learn to accommodate and manage their union daily.

## Husbands, Love your Wives

People of God, perhaps you wonder why God is issuing this divine instruction? First, marriage was established to function as a reflection of the Trinity; the husband is the head and the "president" of the house, the wife is the mother and the "prime minister" of the house and the children are the offspring of the marriage.

As the church was established to function within the Trinitarian concept of God the Father, God the Son, and God the Holy Spirit, so also Jesus is the husband and head of the church. Humans act as the priest and minister in the church, and the Holy Spirit is the comforter, counsellor, and guide. Similarly, a husband and wife ought to function in oneness of body, soul, and spirit.

The greatest value a man can offer his wife and their marriage is love; it releases the fuel to ignite the emotion that produces commitment and submission for a one-flesh union. It guarantees family security and gives a sense of belonging and direction. Jacob gave such value to Rachel even before their marriage was contracted; he agreed to serve an extra seven years of labour in addition to a previous seven years he had already served because of her. Again, when Rachel had delays in becoming pregnant, Jacob never treated her with less value.

As Jacob invested love in Rachel in good and bad seasons, so also God added blessing to the family and Rachel's womb. She later gave birth to the son who carried the mantle of leadership for the household of Jacob.

Husband, place a high value on your wife; invest love into her life and watch how it spreads within the household. Heaven will nurture the love with blessing and prosperity for the family.

What type of man in a marriage is truly a husband? A husband is a man who loves his wife wholeheartedly and unconditionally and is committed to providing security for his wife and children. The man who is faithful to his marriage bond and who gives attention to his wife and children when he is most needed is a true husband.

The Bible says: "Find rest O my soul, in God alone my hope comes from him" (Ps. 62: 5). A husband is a man who can be trusted by his wife, from whom peace and assurance of fulfilled life is guaranteed.

At creation, God shaped the woman perfectly and beautifully so that she would have the characteristics of the rib: strong yet delicate, to provide protection for the most delicate organ in man, his heart. Man's heart is the center of his being, and his lungs hold the breath of life. The rib cage prevents damage to the heart.

Therefore, women were made to support men, just as the rib cage supports the body.

Husbands, how you treat your wife is how you treat God. When you crush her, you only damage your own heart. That is why it is absolutely important for men to love their wives: so that women can support their husbands in humility and with the power of God, each showing to her husband that she will protect his inner self. If you believe and practice this, you will see the glory of God.

God is actively involved in marriage and the church, the institutions He established to serve as extensions of His heavenly government on earth. God said, "Let us create man in our own image according to our likeness and let them rule over" (Gen. 1: 26) and also commanded: "I am the Lord your God, consecrate yourself and be holy because I am Holy" (Lev. 11: 44). What a passionate call from God for man to be like Him. My simple definition of holiness is "obedience to God's commands."

The *New English Dictionary* defines "tripartite" as: "divided into three parts" and the meaning of "triumvirate" is given as: "Joint rule by three men". This is the perfect description of how the Trinity is represented in heaven, marriage, and the church. Jesus said, "I am the vine, you are the branches. If a man remains in me and I in him, he will bear much fruit; apart from me you can do nothing" (John 15: 5). This is also the structure of the Jewish tabernacle: The outer court, the holy court, and the holy of Holies. Also, humans consist of body, soul, and spirit.

Without the involvement of God the Father, Jesus, and the Holy Spirit in marriage, a husband will find it difficult to love his wife unconditionally. Likewise, a wife will not be able to love, honour, and respect her husband. God the Father, Jesus, and the Holy Spirit must be allowed to lead our marriages The Bible says, "Husbands, love your wives even as Christ also loved the Church and gave Himself for her" (Eph. 5: 25).

The love that flows from God to man must also flow from the man to the woman in a household and must be the focus of every Christian or Godly family; it is a divine heritage for the children of God.

# TRIPARTITE TRIUMVIRATE

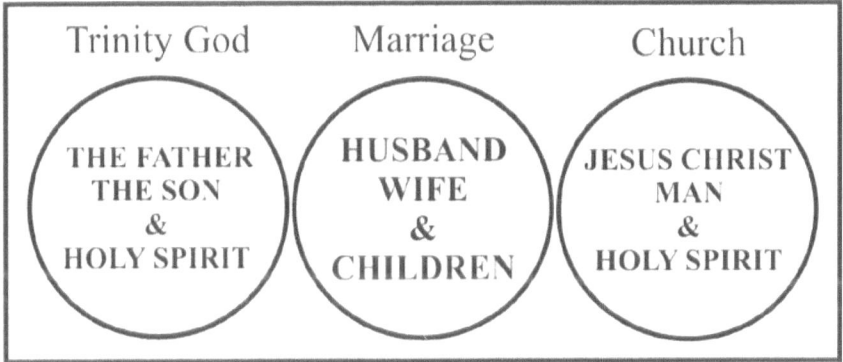

| Trinity God | Marriage | Church |
|---|---|---|
| THE FATHER THE SON & HOLY SPIRIT | HUSBAND WIFE & CHILDREN | JESUS CHRIST MAN & HOLY SPIRIT |

My idea of the divine tripartite triumvirate explains the three tiers of the institutions in which God intervenes directly in the affairs of man.

God reigned from eternity past before creation and remains one with the Son and the Holy Spirit (the members of the Trinity) to create heaven and earth. He breathed His Spirit into the nostrils of man, and man became a living soul in the image and likeness of God (Gen. 1: 27). He saw the need for man not to be alone, so He conducted the first marriage and institutionalised it (Gen. 2: 22–24), upon which He gave rulership and dominion of this world to man (Gen. 1: 28). After humans fell from grace, God offered

His only begotten Son (John 3: 16), who gave his life as a living sacrifice on the cross at Calvary (John 10: 11) and sent the Holy Spirit as promised by God the Father (John 16: 7) to establish the church on the day of Pentecost (Acts 2: 4).

Beloved, the fundamental truth remains that God the Father, the Son, and the Holy Spirit are indivisible, truthful, and faithful from eternity past to eternity future. Regrettably, humans appear to be failing God in virtually every area in which He has poured out His love for us through marriage and the church. The Bible says, "But God commanded His love toward us. In that, while we were yet sinners, Christ died for us" (Rom. 5: 8).

The fact remains that Jesus is coming back soon to take His bride, "the Church". Therefore, the need to restore the institution of marriage is a huge challenge for Christians and the church. I pose this question: are Christians actually taking dominion and ruling over the earth, or have we abdicated? For instance, many nations, including Great Britain, which pioneered spreading the gospel to many nations of the world, appears to have backslidden and compromised God's rules under the guise of human rights arguments. Churches are being sold and converted to pubs or other religious houses with altars built for idols.

Christ loved his church (his wife) and yielded Himself in love as a living sacrifice for her. When He resurrected and ascended to heaven, He sent the Holy Spirit to the church (Acts 2: 4) and gave gifts to man. Paul writes, "It was He who gave some to be Apostles, some to be Prophets, some to be evangelists, some to be pastors and teachers" (Eph. 4: 11).

Agape love flows from God the Father to the Son, to the Holy Spirit, to man, and to the church. Correspondingly, unconditional love from the heart of the husband should flow to the wife, and it will automatically affect the entire household to provoke blessing, prosperity, success, peace, longevity, and an uncommon testimony.

God, through Apostle Paul, issued this commandment to all husbands. It is not advice or a suggestion but an instruction that must be obeyed. God made it mandatory for husbands to love their wives sacrificially and unconditionally. Until a man loves his wife as Christ Jesus loves His church, he is not walking in agreement with the word of God. Christ shows His love for the church not only when she obeys him but also when she offends him. The Bible says, "But God commanded His love toward us. In that, while we were yet sinners, Christ died for us" (Rom. 5: 8).

God instructs that a man should love his wife despite her shortcomings and errors. Until he complies with this commandment, there may not be fulfilment in the family. Therefore, a man should seek God's help to rekindle love for his wife in his heart, according to God's word. The love for one's wife must come after the love of God and it must be expressed. Regarding this, Paul writes, "So ought men to love their wives as their own bodies. He that loved his wife loved himself. For no man ever yet hated his own flesh; but nourished and cherished his body even as the Lord the Church" (Eph. 5: 28–29).

Accordingly, every husband should love their wives unconditionally. Otherwise, the devil may give her negative ideas, like he did with Eve. When husbands express their love to their wives, they are likely to see her good virtues manifested. No woman hates to be loved

## Various Character Traits of Husbands

| 1. | **Bachelor Husband** | They love to do things on their own without consulting their wives; they love to hang out with their friends a lot rather than their wife and children. |
|---|---|---|
| 2. | **Acidic Husband** | These husbands are always angry, moody, violent, and dominating. |
| 3. | **Slave Husband** | These are husbands who always want to be treated like kings and treat their wives like slaves. They want their wives to treat them with traditional gestures of respect. They don't like to be called by their first name. |
| 4, | **General Husband** | These men act like a husband to every woman. They love and care for women other than their own wives; they like giving money to other women instead of giving it to their wives. They have many female friends. |
| 5. | **Panadol Husband** | These men use their wives as problem solvers. This kind of husband loves his wife when he needs something from her, and after that, she becomes useless to him. He is clever at understanding the woman's weaknesses and capitalises on them to get what he wants from his wife. |

| 6. | **Dry Husband** | These are moody and stingy men. Their sex is dry; they are in and out and suddenly leave their wives dry and sore emotionally. They don't put energy into the relationship to make it enjoyable. |
|----|-----------------|---|
| 7. | **Parasite Husband** | They are lazy men who don't work, so they cling to their wives' money. They act like loving husbands, but they eventually use their wives' resources to cheat on her. |
| 8 | **Baby Husband** | These men are very irresponsible and childish; they cannot make decisions without asking for advice from their mother or other relatives. They often rush back to their parents with issues instead of discussing and reaching a conclusion with their wives; this kind of man always wants his wife to care for him as his mother did. |
| 9 | **Visiting Husband** | These are men who are always at work. They come home as if they are visiting; they do provide for the needs of their wives, but they are not always at home with their families. |
| 10 | **Good Husband** | These are caring and loving men who always provide for the material and emotional needs of their families, they always make time for their families and guide their home spiritually. They are very responsible and trustworthy, and they treat their wives as partners. |

## Various Character Traits of Wives

| 1. | Party Wife | These are women who are very mobile and sociable; they are always attending one function after the other. They are barely at home on weekends to spend time with their husbands and families. |
|----|------------|------------------------------------------------------------|
| 2. | Dictionary Wife | These are women who don't take suggestions; they believe that the way they think is the way things must be done. They are very orderly and easily get angry when things are misplaced in their home. |
| 3. | Pampered Wife | These women were spoiled by their parents, normally from a rich family, or they are the only girls among boys in the family. They are lazy, they hardly do household work and they love spending money and seeing their husband as a houseboy. |
| 4. | Office Wife | These are career-minded women with the mind-set that their family does not matter; they always use their career as an excuse for not being at home. They don't respect their husband and make educated women look bad. They believe that their husband is not important because they can afford to take care of themselves. |

| 5. | **Patient Wife** | These women always look like they are sick and downtrodden; they love complaining about their husband, children, relatives, and the weather. They live in fear and anxiety. |
|---|---|---|
| 6. | **Headmistress Wife** | These are women who place themselves in charge of the family even when the husband is the sole provider of the home. They treat everyone as a child, including their husbands and visitors. They are too inquisitive and will punish their husbands over every trivial issue. |
| 7. | **Boxing Wife** | These are women who are very offensive and aggressive and sometimes can be very violent; they like shouting and nagging and sometimes believe in trading fire for fire. |
| 8. | **Dustbin Wife** | These wives are very dirty, unkempt, disorganised, and confused. They are lazy at everything except gossiping and eating; they leave everything for their husbands and children to do. |

| 9. | **Security Wife** | They are women who are very protective of their husbands; they are very jealous and see every woman as a threat. They consider their husbands' friends to be bad company, and they will not allow anyone to discipline their children. These women's husbands, families, friends, and colleagues are often scared of them. |
|---|---|---|
| 10. | **Good Wife** | These women are virtuous, caring, loving, and very smart. They are very helpful and can handle their family business effectively in the absence of their husbands; these wives also provide spiritual guidance for their husbands and the children and are very understanding and full of self-esteem. |

## The Virtuous Woman

Let's establish the identity of a virtuous woman as we consider the nature of the woman created by God. A woman is created with a womb, to incubate a new life until it is mature enough to be delivered. Women tend to be emotional and have gentle, caring, and submissive hearts.

Who is a virtuous woman? In Proverbs 31: 10–30, the Bible lists all the attributes of a virtuous woman. She is described as a wife of a noble character; her worth is above rubies. Therefore, a virtuous woman is the married woman who dutifully performs her God-given responsibilities.

A wife of noble character who can find? She is worth more than rubies; her husband has full confidence in her and lacks nothing of value. She brings him good not harm all the days of her life. She selects wool and flax and works with eager hands. She is like merchant's ship bringing her food from afar. She get up while it is still dark, she provides food for her family. And portion for her servant girls. She considers a field and buys it; out of her earning she plants a vineyard. She sets about her works vigorously; her arms are strong for her tasks. She sees that her trading is profitable and her lamp does not go out at night. In her hands she holds the distaff and grasps the spindle with her fingers. She extends her hands to the needy. When it is snow, she has no fear for her household; for all of them are clothed in scarlet. She makes covering for her bed; she is clothed in fine linen and purple. Her husband is respected at the city gate when he takes his seat among the elders of the land. She makes the linen garments and sells them, and supplies the merchant with sashes. She is clothed with strength and dignity, she can laugh at the days to come. She speaks with wisdom and faithful instruction is on her tongue. She watches over the affairs of her household and does not eat the bread of idleness. Her children arise and call her blessed; her husband also and he praises her. Many women do noble things but you surpass them all. Charm is deceptive, and beauty is fleeting; but a woman who fears the Lord is to be praised. Give her the reward she has earned and let her works bring her praises at the city gate. (Prov. 31: 10–31 NIV)

Her virtues are defined as: morality excellence, admirable quality, beauty, and good habits of the soul. A virtuous woman is the governor of her home, the live wire of her family. Her responsibility is to bring all the family members under a shield of love, peace, and harmony and give the daily strength of love to the president of the house, the husband and father, so he succeeds and prospers in all things.

A virtuous woman is the wife whose heart's desire is to honour God with all her being and to bring God's glory in the family.

A woman does not simply wake up and blossom into a virtuous woman overnight. Becoming a virtuous woman is a process that takes determination, interaction with the Holy Spirit, and daily inspiration from the scriptures, as she is supported with love from her husband. Therefore, let's consider the inner qualities of the wonderful wife, called a virtuous woman.

## Her Possessions and quality.

1. She is trustworthy (v. 11).
2. She is a positive influence. (v. 12).
3. She is a hard worker (v.13, 14, 19, 24–27).
4. She is a planner (v. 21–22).
5. She is protective (v. 27).
6. She is dependable.
7. She is a great witness to those around her.
8. She is wise.

## Her Achievements

1.  She meets the needs of her home (v. 15).
2.  She invests for her household (v. 16).
3.  She keeps herself in shape (v. 17).
4.  She helps her husband become successful (v. 23).

## Her Attitudes: Happy and content

1.  She is delightful (v. 13).
2.  She is healthy (v. 18).
3.  She is compassionate (v. 20).
4.  She is unselfish (v. 20).
5.  She is honest (v. 25).
6.  She fears God (v.31).
7.  She is kind and generous.
8.  She cares for her husband and children.

## Her Applause

1.  Her family applauds her (v. 28).
2.  Her husband applauds her (v. 28–29).
3.  She fears the Lord (v. 30)
4.  God's word applauds her (v. 30).
5.  Her works bring her applause from people (v. 31).

What does the fear of the Lord mean? According to *Strong's Concordance*, fear means "reverence". She lives her life for the Lord; she loves the Lord, and she does everything to His glory! She is truthful and faithful.

Women, some of you may doubt your ability to measure up to this virtuous woman, and you may have said in your hearts, "It is too difficult to be like this virtuous woman, especially in today's society." Certainly, you can be one amongst millions. Jesus has a response for this feeling of doubt But Jesus looked at them and said: 'With man this is impossible, but with God nothing shall be impossible'" (Matt. 19: 26 NIV). You too could be one of the virtuous women in history, if only you desire to be one. Jesus said, "Come unto me all who are heavy laden and I will give you rest. Take my yoke upon you and learn from me for I am gentle and humble in heart, you will find rest for your souls. For my yoke is easy and my burden is light" (Matt. 11: 28–30).

Women, you're the life of your home; you have the holy gifts to secure the love of your husbands. Tell God your aspirations; He will not deny you your heart's desires. Wives, you can be like this virtuous woman in Proverbs 31 and be a great witness to your household, to your husband, and to those around you. Be determined that you want people to see Jesus in you and be transformed to be a virtuous woman. Jesus said, "If anyone would come after me, he must deny himself and take up his cross and follow me" (Matt. 16: 24 NIV). Wives, be willing to be the virtuous woman of your age. You can do it.

The virtue of a woman is found not in her outward beauty but in her beautiful character, holy manners, and mutual submissiveness, as the governor of the home, to her husband, who is the president of the house.

The Bible says "Wives, in the same way be submissive to your husbands so that, if any of them do not believe the word, they may be won over without words by the behaviour of their wives, when they see the purity and reverence of your lives,. Your beauty should not come from outward adornment, such as braided hair and the wearing of gold jewellery and fine clothes. Instead, it should be that of your inner self, the unfading beauty of a gentle and quiet spirit, which is of great worth in God's sight" (1 Pet. 3: 1–4 NIV).

## Christian Marriage and Obligations

Do you ever wonder what the scene was like the first night Adam met his wife, Eve, in the delightful and pleasurable garden at Eden? It must have been a beautiful and picturesque place to say the least, not polluted by sin or vulgar imagination.

God must have been pleased to see that the first couple, Adam and Eve, were comfortable in the garden He created. At that time, the act of Christian marriage held its greatest appeal and the pre-eminent position in any environment. The world tried to emulate this environment, with the tradition of newlywed couples going on a honeymoon. This idea was initiated by God in the garden of Eden, and it has been borrowed from the Church by many communities around the world.

Every couple should make every intimate moment with each other honourable, unique, and memorable. The bedroom environment must be neat, beautiful, and attractive; all relationships must be seen as being God's project and for His glory.

Both partners should realise that using perfume (or cologne) and deodorants improves their experience with each other. We must genuinely care for each other. Wives must learn to appeal to their husbands. Make the home heaven on earth, and help your husband to appreciate you at all times.

Christian wives should make the act of sex attractive for their husbands and create an exciting atmosphere. Let your husband feel comfortable. Do not use the Christian life as an excuse to deny your husband of intimacy with you.

The husband should fulfil his marital duty to his wife and likewise the wife to her husband. The wife's body does not belong to her alone but also to her husband; in the same way, the husband's body does not belong to him alone but also to his wife. Do not deprive each other of sex except by mutual consent and for a time so that you may devote yourself to prayer. Then come together again so that Satan will not tempt you because of your lack of control (1 Cor. 7: 3–5).

No wonder the beloved spouse of Solomon took time to make herself a delight.

> You have stolen my heart, my sister, my pride; you have stolen my heart with one glance of my eyes, with one jewel of your necklace. How delightful is your love my sister, my bride! How much more pleasing is your love than wine, and the fragrance of your perfume than any spice! Your lips drop sweetness as the honeycomb my bride; milk and honey are under your tongue. The fragrance of your garment is like that of Lebanon. You are a garden locked up, my sister, my bride, you are a spring enclosed, a sealed fountain. Your plants are an orchard of pomegranates with choice fruits, with henna and nard, nard and saffron, calamus and cinnamon with every kind of incense tree, with myrrh and aloes and all the finest spices. You are a garden fountain, a well of flowing water streaming down from Lebanon. Awake, north wind, and

come, south wind! Blow on my garden that its
fragrance may spread abroad. Let my lover come
into his garden and taste its choice fruits. (S. of S.
4: 9–16).

It is not surprising that the man in this passage yearned to come
into his beloved garden and eat pleasant fruits. She prepared
herself and her environment for him. Like I said earlier, wives are
the governors of homes; they have the key to make the home more
appealing for their husband.

The husband's sexual appetite determines the frequency of sexual
relations in marriage. If his sex drive is low, look for a solution
in prayer and by consulting experts. Sex is the lubricant for love;
don't overlook that in your marriage. It helps the couple grow and
mature together in spirit as they fulfil this gift of love from God
to strengthen their marriage.

As mentioned earlier, God's primary motive for establishing the
marriage institution is companionship. It precluded a conjugal
relationship between husbands and wives. The Bible directs that
wives should not deny their husbands access to their body and
likewise the husband. God knows that man cannot wait for too
long without having sex. He knows that men could dabble in
adultery if prevented from having sex with their wives, hence the
above injunction.

Even in a proper, lawful sexual relationship between husband and
wife, Satan may tempt members of a couple through their sexual
desires if they denied themselves sex and do not take absolute care
to prevent temptation.. So, the primary obligation in a marriage is
to satisfy the sexual desires of both the husband and wife.

## Fidelity in Marriage

What do we mean by fidelity in marriage? It is the quality of reliability and trustworthiness to one's partner. Being faithful is not a favour you bestow on your spouse. It is a privilege to bless yourself with.

The prevalent culture in the world today suggests to people that the pursuit of personal pleasure surpasses all other considerations. Fidelity in marriage has become a casualty of this paradigm. The significance of marriage, which was considered the building block of society that bound spouses together in physical, mental, emotional, and spiritual oneness has become a marginalised concept.

In Christian marriage, fidelity doesn't happen automatically. It involves commitment, acceptance, and mutual respect, bonded together with love and fear of God. Spouses set themselves apart from all others and give themselves exclusively to each other. Christian marriage is based on the reciprocity principle. These partners, who have pledged to love each other "till death do us part", must work at it actively and continuously. There is no casual break or vacation written into the contract. Scripture includes examples of such a faithful bond, such as the following one from Ruth.

> Entreat me not to leave thee or to return from following after thee, for whither thou goest I will go and where thou lodgest I will lodge, thy people shall be my people and thy God my God, where thou diest will I die, and there will I be buried; the Lord do so to me and more also if ought but death part thee and me. (Ruth 1: 16–17 KJV)

The world is in the grip of a sexual revolution; sexual exploits and pornography are displayed in the print, Internet, and electronic media. The attendant consequences, which include the wrath of God, are visible all over the world. Fidelity in marriage demands that you adhere to the marriage bond.

Husbands and wives are to develop the spirit of togetherness and total abstinence from casual sex, come rain or come sunshine. They must resolve themselves to tackle all obstacles together. Each day should be one in which couples yearn to draw from the well of vows they made. These vows are real-life vows. When you vowed to love your spouse, did you ever imagine that some people don't know how to receive love and that your spouse may be one of them? How could you have known? You just love them! The remedy is to be willing to learn how to love your spouse in the way the Bible teaches us about love: "If I speak in the tongues of men and of angels, but have not love, I am only a resounding gong or a clanging cymbal" (1 Cor. 13: 1). We are all in a classroom, and the earlier we are ready to join hands and grow together, the better our marriages will be.

In marriage, there are various challenges because you are totally different people, with different upbringings and temperaments, yet you would like to spend the rest of your lives together.

The willingness to journey together in sickness and health, for better, for worse, for richer and for poorer, with or without food, and standing by what you vowed is the well from which you draw strength to live together honourably. One may wonder, how do I protect my spouse – from what and whom? This means your spouse's enemies become your enemies too.

You protect your spouse from things that want to devour what you are building in your marriage regarding communication, trust, intimacy, and other value systems. You may also protect them from in-laws who don't honour or respect them, and you even protect them from yourself – your ego and selfishness.

Forsaking all other women or men means that irrespective of your close friends, your spouse is a priority in all you do. See to it that his or her needs are attended to. Secondly, be faithful. The high rate of divorce has its roots in infidelity, which causes grief and heartbreak. As people who know the Lord, our marriages should always reflect the honour that God calls couples to in marriage.

## Christian Faith and Social Morality

Most Christians have no difficulty in seeing the implications of faith for our private lives. We know that we are called to love our neighbours as ourselves, but we are tempted to limit that love to the neighbours who are close and personally known to us. We see moral issues that arise in family life, such as drug abuse, sexual activity, pornography, and dishonesty, but we tend to view the world outside our immediate environment as secular and therefore do not concern ourselves with addressing the issues. Behaviour in those realms is governed by abstractions of the laws of economics, the realities of politics or human nature. In some parts of the world, Christians call for justice and humanity in the marketplace or in law-enforcement agencies; these people are often regarded as naive meddlers, out of place in the world. However, we should not be afraid of being called names because our religious tradition bears witness to another way of thinking.

For example, the prophets in the land of Israel were as vigorous in their denunciation of economic evil as they were in condemning idolatry. They denounced land-grabbing, political injustice, bribery, and the alliances of their kings with other nations.

Jesus observed that it is hard for the rich to enter into the kingdom of God. The book of Revelation calls the Roman Empire the whore of Babylon; the medieval church taught the importance of paying and receiving a just price and avoiding the evil of usury.

The Christian cannot, therefore, suspend ethical judgement when entering the social world. Our behaviours as citizens, workers, consumers, and professionals are part of our total Christian life for which we are accountable to God. The Christians are to lead politics to determine the nation's ethical and economic behaviours. We are to steer the affairs of nations in the direction of God. Our failure in this regard is an indication that we have abdicated our throne for earthly rulership. Consequently, the moral issues and disorders in society have permeated the institution of marriage and are threatening families.

## Sacredness of Marriage

We need to recognise that if our marriages ever stray significantly away from the moral, spiritual, and ethical principles of the Bible, then our families will be doomed. This is the greatest wisdom needed to maintain the sacredness of marriage.

Observations in social science clearly document the fact that the breakdown of the traditional two-parent, biological husband-and-wife family is a major factor contributing to the overall moral, religious, and ethical decline of all nations.

Our Lord Jesus Christ advised the teachers of the law that "Moses, because of the hardness of your heart suffered you to put away your wives but from the beginning it was not so and I say unto you whosoever shall put his wife away except it be for fornication and shall marry another, commit adultery, and whosoever shall marry her that is divorced committed adultery (Matt. 19: 8–9).

And the Apostle Paul says, "To the married I give this command (not I but the Lord); A wife must not separate from her husband, but if she does, she must remain unmarried or else be reconciled with her husband. And a husband must not divorce his wife" (1 Cor. 7: 10–11) NIV.

The fact remains that God, who is in heaven (Dan. 2: 28), has spoken to the human race through His inspired written word in the Bible, and He has designed the structure of society in Love. He created male and female with the intention for one man to marry one woman for life.

God intended for husbands and wives to produce children who, in turn, receive nurturing care from their parents in a stable and loving home. Paul writes, "Wives, submit to your husbands, as is fitting in the Lord. Husbands, love your wives and do not be harsh with her. Children, obey your parents in everything, for this pleases the Lord. Father, do not embitter your children, or they will be discouraged" (Col. 3: 18–21).

In another letter, Paul also says, "Children, obey your parents in the Lord, for this is right. Honour your father and mother which is the first commandment with a promise, that it may go well with you and that you may enjoy long life on the earth. Father, do not exasperate your children, instead bring them up in the training and instruction of the Lord" (Eph. 6: 1–4). In the divinely ordained institution of the home, God intended that children receive the necessary instruction and training to prepare them to be productive, honest, God-fearing, hard-working citizens. Regrettably, some parents leave violence, hatred, bitterness, adultery, and other vices for their children as a heritage. The home environment was designed by God to impart each succeeding generation with proper Christian moral and social principles that would in turn make their nation strong and virtuous.

The Bible is filled with references to the essential ingredients of healthy family life and proper parenting skills; some of these instructions are found in Deuteronomy 4: 7–9; 6: 1–9; 32: 46–47; Psalm 127; Proverbs 5: 15–20; 6: 20–35 and Proverbs 13: 24; 19: 18; 23: 13–14.

> For the woman which hath husband is bound by the law to her husband so long as he liveth, but then if the husband is dead, she is loosed from the law of the husband, so then if while her husband liveth she be married to another man shall be called adulteress. But if her husband be dead she is free from the law so that she is no adulteress, though she be married to another man. (Rom. 7: 2–3)

## Marriage: An Honourable Estate

Marriage is an honourable estate, and God's desire is for each couple to live a covenant life; that is, you live each day in line with what you vowed to your spouse. You vowed to love, protect and comfort him or her, forsaking all others. The Bible says, "Marriage should be honoured by all and the marriage bed kept pure, for God will judge the adulterer and all the sexually immoral" (Heb. 13: 4).

Couples are advised to avoid doubting their marriage no matter how difficult things could be. Do not give up hope on becoming victorious, as a couple, over whatever situation or difficulty you may be passing through. With God, all things are possible.

**Righteousness exalts a nation (Proverbs 14:34). Pray for your marriage to be a foundation of righteousness and your family to be a pillar of a righteous nation. Build your home on the rock as a dwelling place for the Holy Spirit, where God desire to establish His glory forever.**

## Chapter Four

# CHARACTERISTICS OF THE IDEAL CHRISTIAN FAMILY

### Family Values

W hat exactly makes up a strong family that possesses good values? A strong family supports and nourishes its members throughout the lifespan of that family.

Family values are traditionally the foundation upon which children learn how to grow into maturity. Your family values consist of moral and spiritual ideas passed down from generation to generation to produce leaders of a nation.

## Faith

A successful Christian marriage requires a couple to have faith in themselves and in God to manage and sustain their family. Fear disappears where faith resides, and without faith, we cannot please God (Heb. 11: 6). The Bible says, "Now faith is being sure of what we hope for and certain of what we do not see" (Heb. 11: 1).

Family faith must begin with the married couple trusting and obeying God; they must have faith in Him as the Alpha and Omega who provides for their needs, according to His riches in glory. God will protect the family even when they are going through the valley of the shadow of death. God is the Good Shepherd, who leads believers besides the still waters to restore their soul (Ps. 23: 2–4).

Having faith in God entails seeing God as our Father who will always lead us beside the still waters to restore our souls (Ps. 23: 2–3) and not suffer our feet to be moved (Ps 121: 3a). Faith and hope in God is about laying all the family burdens on Him in prayer, with definite assurance that He will fix the problem and grant all noble desires.

## Honour and Respect

In the *Collins English Dictionary*, synonyms of 'honour' and 'respect' include: dignify, exalt, glorify, grace, revere, venerate, adore, hallow, civility, esteem, dignity, reputation, magnanimity, nobleness, and more. These virtues should be visible among Christian married couples. Spouses should understand the importance of demonstrating honour and respect for each other. Practicing these values within the household will activate the indwelling royal attributes we possess as children of God. It also ignites blessing, success, and prosperity.

All humans have elements of dignity and nobleness inside which can only manifest themselves when couples honour and respect each other. When you dishonour and disrespect your spouse with negative attitudes and provocative words, you're provoking anger and irrational behaviour from your spouse, but when you both respect and honour each other, you are provoking the royal qualities inside your spouse to rise to the surface. Beloved husband and wife, call out the spirit of prince and princess or king and queen in your spouse by relating to each other in honour and respect.

Adam valued his wife Eve and called her "bone of my bone and flesh of my flesh." Only a well-brought-up prince will regard and call his wife a princess; likewise, a woman who was raised properly will call her husband a prince. The values of honour and respect among husbands and wives are the gold in the family household: not visible to a fool but very obvious to a wise person. Dig it out, refine it, and it will add great value to your family.

## Family Prayer Altar

Your heart is the spiritual altar where the Holy Spirit dwells (Gal. 5: 16–17). Similarly, the family altar is a dedicated place for worship and fellowship with the Lord within the family home. Prayer is the communication channel between man and God, initiated by the Holy Spirit in the hearts of God's people and conveyed by the Holy Spirit to the throne of God. "In the same way, the Spirit helps us in our weakness. We do not know what we ought to pray for, but the Spirit himself intercedes for us with groans that words cannot express. And He who searches our hearts knows the mind of the Spirit, because the Spirit intercedes for the saints in accordance with God's will" (Rom. 8: 26–27 NIV).

The Holy Spirit brings a believer's mind into perfect harmony with God during prayer and sends it not merely as a human desire but as a divine prayer. A believer's prayer does not remain the voice of man crying to God; it becomes the voice of God expressing the needs of His children and conveying them to the throne to obtain answers for blessing, healing, deliverance, and prosperity.

> Ask it shall be given to you, seek, and you will find; knock and the door will be opened to you. For everyone who asks receives; he who seeks finds; and to him who knocks, the door will be opened. Which of you, if his son asks for bread, will give him a stone? Or if he asks for fish, will give him a snake? (Matt. 7: 7–10 NIV)

God ordained prayer as the means of communication with Him to accomplish a mission that He has promised to finish. We pray not because the outcome of our request is uncertain but because God has promised and cannot fail.

Fight for your peace in prayer; fight for divine love within the family circle and your community. Fight for your financial breakthrough in prayer. Fight for divine health and healing. Fight for wisdom, knowledge, and understanding in prayer. Fight for unique testimonies for your family and over all issues within the family. Fight in prayer against all evil, ancestral altars where missiles from demonic and witchcraft origins have been launched against your destiny and family. All of these things will be established through prayer.

Beloved, your destiny is in your own hands. The scripture says; the kingdom of God suffered violent and it is taken by force (Matt. 11: 12). Don't allow the devil to tamper with any aspect of your destiny; fight back with prayer and fasting.

Prayer is like an assuring electric field connecting heaven and earth; when the field sparks, the matter is taken care of. "For the weapons of our warfare are not carnal, but mighty through God to the pulling down of strongholds" (2 Cor. 10: 4). Therefore, all Christian families are to use prayer as a weapon to fight and defeat the enemy and his fallen angels (i.e., demons). Families must pray to obtain their freedom and possess what is theirs. Prayer is the key to overcoming all obstacles and defeating the devil.

To limit of Satan's power in our families, we must join the will of God together with family desires in prayers. When the sovereignty of God is linked to the obedience of man, the will of God is put into effect, and Satan is defeated.

Plead the blood of Jesus over the entire household and all its belongings. Take the authority of the word of God, the power of the blood of Jesus, and the anointing of the Holy Spirit to bind demons and recover what the devil has stolen from you and your ancestors. Pray ceaselessly with fire, but, husbands and wives, beware of that monster called unsettled conflict. If allowed, it will fester and grow in size, hindering your prayers from being answered. Husbands, be quick to settle all conflicts with your wives; be at peace with each other before you approach your prayer altar; wives should do likewise. The Bible says, "Husbands, in the same way, be considerate as you live with your wives and treat them with respect as the weaker partner and as heirs with you of the gracious gift of life, so that nothing will hinder your prayers" (1 Pet. 3: 7).

## Deliverance

Deliverance is advisable for everyone afflicted with sickness, disease, failure, poverty, stagnation, limitation, rejection, and all manners of negative tendencies, including those who are demonically possessed. Deliverance is done through the knowledge of the word of God, the use of the blood of Jesus Christ, and the Holy Spirit. The Bible says, "But on Mount Zion will be deliverance, it will be holy, and the house of Jacob will possess their possession" (Obad. 1: 17 NIV). Deliverance is meant to remove yokes of affliction and destroy every burden (Isa. 10: 27 NIV).

Deliverance is the enforcement of heavenly authority upon the devil and his cohorts to set the captive free and restore all that has been stolen, destroyed, and killed in someone's life by the devil.

Demonic affliction causes barrenness, sickness, disease, failure, setback, stagnancy, poverty, strife, marriage dissolution, hatred, bitterness, waywardness, drunkenness, and other negative manifestations of the devil's work in the family. In fact, deliverance is the essence of Christ's ministry on earth and His death on the cross of Calvary. It is the purpose of the church and a significant reason for the gift of the Holy Spirit. The Bible says, "Upon mount Zion, there shall be deliverance and it shall be holy and the household of Jacob shall possess their possession" (Obad. 1: 17).

This wonderful message was addressed to the household of Jacob to emphasise three key points about deliverance: the promises of (1) deliverance, (2) holiness, and (3) possessing our possessions. Specifically, the devil always tries to becloud human life with ungodliness so that he can steal, destroy, and kill whatever blessing God has given to man. Deliverance, therefore, demands purging ourselves of ungodliness and evil manifestations to facilitate possessing our possessions.

A prophesy in the book of Isaiah declares, "The Spirit of the Sovereign Lord is upon me because the Lord has anointed me to preach good news to the poor, He has sent me to bind up the broken hearted, to proclaim freedom for the captives and release from darkness for the prisoner" (Isa. 61: 1 NIV).

The meaning of "freedom for the captives and release from darkness for the prisoner" is, put simply, deliverance. When things turn negative, when love suddenly turns to hatred, when a financial situation takes a downward dive, we need deliverance to be set free from the devourer, Satan, and from generational curses. When sweetness turns to bitterness, when misunderstanding and misbehaviour prevails within the household, and when the fruit of the marriage suddenly turns negative, your approach must be to pursue prayer and deliverance, not separation or divorce.

Jesus's ministry, from the beginning to His victory on the cross at Calvary, is about proclaiming and bringing deliverance for humanity. The Bible says, "Jesus went throughout Galilee, teaching in their synagogues, preaching the good news of the Kingdom and healing every disease and sickness among the people. News about him (Jesus) spread all over Syria and people brought to him all who were ill with various diseases, those suffering severe pain, the demon possessed, those having seizures, and the paralysed, and he healed them (Matt. 4: 23–24).

Jesus Christ gave believers (disciples) the authority, through deliverance, to be set the captive free from the devil's manipulation, affliction, and invasion of people's lives (Matt. 10: 1) The Bible says, "I tell you the truth, whatever you bind on earth will be bound in heaven, and whatever you loose on earth will be loosed in heaven" (Matt 18: 18). These passages from Matthew record a time when Jesus Christ commissioned and sent out his disciples to carry out healing and deliverance. Speaking on this topic another time, Jesus says, "And this signs shall accompany those who believe: in my name they will drive out demons (deliverance); they will speak in tongues; they will pick up snakes with their hands; and when they drink deadly poison, it will not hurt them at all; they will lay their hands on sick people and they will get hill" (Mark 16: 17–18).

In the Old Testament, Joshua was a high priest who was always in the presence of God, yet he was clothed with filthy garment by the devil to prevent him from attaining his spiritual potential. The Bible says the angels of the Lord intervened in deliverance, and the filthy garments were removed. Joshua was clothed with garments and a turban of honour so he could actualise his spiritual potential (Zech. 3: 1–7).

Friends, the devil is not prepared to spare anyone. The Bible warns that "we should be alert and be vigilant because our accuser, the devil, is a roaring lion walking up and down seeking for whom he may devour" (1 Pet. 5: 8). You can never tell when the devil penetrates your family members through gluttony or sexually immoral thoughts or through other legal grounds. Your weapon against the devil is prayer and deliverance, using the word of God, the blood of Jesus, and the anointing of Holy Spirit.

Jesus called the devil a thief who will not seek permission to enter your house. Thieves are unwelcome guests who invade the house to steal what rightfully belongs to the owner. During an invasion, thieves destroy whatever possible to gain access to the house they intend to rob. They shoot and kill whoever stands in their way. That is exactly how the devil operates to invade human lives. The devil is a spirit; he does not have a body of his own. He moves and searches for available bodies of anyone who gives him legal grounds through sins like sexual immorality, idolatry, witchcraft, rebellion, lying, deception, anger and murder etc. (Galatians 5:19-21

The Bible says, "We do not wrestle against flesh and blood, but against principalities, against powers, against the rulers of the darkness of this age, against spiritual hosts of wickedness in the heavenly places" (Eph. 6: 12). Principalities are entities sitting with Satan, assigned to various continents of the world to implement satanic strategies on how to deal with humanity. Powers are entities assigned to influence men and women in authority to obey their instructions. These two divisions of Satan's servants only succeed with the support and the activities of witchcraft, a type of spiritual wickedness in the high places.

The agenda of the witchcraft department in the kingdom of the devil is to make sure that humanity is available for destruction; hence, their operation reaches and operates at the grass-roots level of the human race, and the family is its major target. Sometimes a whole community is affected by the wicked and destructive activities of the agents of witchcraft.

Satan knows that the family is the pivot of society and seeks to capture it through his deceptive manipulations. Once this is achieved, families and societies find it very difficult to achieve their potentials.

Witchcraft is behind every type of bondage, affliction, torment and demonic influence. It is the cruellest department in the kingdom of devil. Witchcraft is the enemy of mankind's destiny; once it is present in a family, deliverance is the answer.

Witchcraft is the special department in Satan's kingdom charged with the responsibility to manipulate the minds of humankind; this clearly shows the subtle character of Satan and manifests his real nature, an undercover wicked being. When witchcraft possesses someone in a family, it begins to manipulate the minds of family members against each other to make sure that the household does not have peace. In the case of a couple, this manipulation could ultimately cause separation and divorce.

When Satan and his demons possess the bodies of people, they cause havoc through affliction that wrecks lives and destroys destinies. Be alert and be vigilant.

From the very beginning of Jesus's ministry, our Lord steadily practiced aggressive warfare against the powers of darkness. He gave the same authority to His disciples, as mentioned previously (Matt. 10: 1; 18: 18). Jesus's main objective during His ministry on earth was conquering the prince of this world so that He could redeem the captives and put the devil to shame (Col. 2: 14–15). For this purpose He came to the world (Luke 4: 18), and on the eve of the cross, He was able to say, "Now shall the prince of this world be cast out" (John 12: 31).

Every family of believers must develop the habit of using the authority through prayer given by our Lord Jesus Christ to bind and cast the devil and his demons out of their lives.

Satan's power in our marriages is limited when we join our faith with God in prayer and practice deliverance. When the sovereignty of God is linked to the obedience of man, Satan is defeated.

## Forgiveness

The heaviest burden a person can carry in his heart is an unforgiving spirit; unforgiveness is a toxic or spiritual poison that destroys the foundation of life's blessing and prosperity while forgiveness restores all losses and heals every wound. The Lord's Prayer refers to the significance of forgiveness: "And forgive us our sins as we forgive those who trespassed against us" (Matt. 6: 12).

We always face a crisis of forgiveness when somebody hurts us unfairly, especially if it is our husband or wife. Choosing to forgive is the loving remedy to be used when we are wronged by a person we trusted and expected to treat us right. The miracle of healing takes place when one person feels the pain and forgives the person who wounded him or her.

The act of forgiving, by itself, is a wonderfully simple act, but it always happens inside a storm of complex emotions. It is the most complex in personal relationships. Forgiveness is a vital tool to disarm and defeat satanic manipulation and to destroy seeds of discord within the family. Forgiveness guarantees unity, rekindles love, and helps actualise family dreams. It is also necessary to extend forgiveness to others before obtaining forgiveness from God to secure blessings and eternal life.

Fellowship and mutual relationships at a human level are restored through forgiveness. Any refusal to forgive and be reconciled to each other is a sin which bars us from receiving God's forgiveness. The Lord says, "For if you forgive men when they sin against you, your heavenly father will also forgive you, but if you do not forgive men their sins, your father will not forgive your sins" (Matt. 6: 14–15).

Unforgiveness is a monster that must be pulled down by Christian families; it stores up every negative action and error of a spouse and blinds the minds of couples from seeing the positive sides of each other. Unforgiveness gives constant reminders of someone's individual shortcomings and errors. In contrast, love will not keep a record of wrongs but instead overlook errors and mistakes. Beloved, as you read this book, remember that humankind disobeyed God and did abominable things against Him, yet He turned Himself into a man in Jesus Christ and made His dwelling among us. He offered Himself as a living sacrifice on the cross to forgive us of our sins.

God did not forgive our sins because we're perfect or sinless but because He loved us unconditionally. Husbands and wives, forgive one another as an act of love, and don't allow bitterness to take root in your families. This is the will of God for you and your marriage. There is no perfect husband or wife on earth; but determination and oneness of purpose will allow you to succeed in marriage. Vengeance makes marriage brutal, but forgiveness improves and strengthens it. Practicing forgiveness heals broken hearts and renews hope. Forgiveness is a reflection of the true nature of God. It indicates a loving heart and is a demonstration of God's Spirit.

Forgiveness is also mandatory for everyone to become a true, born-again child of the heavenly kingdom. According to Christ's instructions, Christians are the sons of God, and a son is to obey his father and follow in his father's footsteps. Therefore, Christian sonship (or daughterhood) means practicing sacrificial love, evidenced by loving one's enemies and praying for one's persecutors. The Bible says, "You have heard that it was said 'Love your neighbour and hate your enemy. But I tell you, Love your enemies and pray for those who persecute you, that you may be sons of your Father in heaven. He causes his sun to rise on the evil and the good and sends rain on the righteous and the unrighteous" (Matt. 5: 43–45).

Forgiveness is the predecessor to agape love. When you forgive someone for hurting you, you perform spiritual surgery to your soul and cut away the wrong done to you so that you can see him or her through a healed soul and new eyes. Forgiveness detaches the hurt from the heart and lets it go, in the same way a child opens his or her hands and lets a trapped butterfly go free. Forgive those who trespass against you, that your sins can be forgiven (Matt. 6: 14–15).

Human fellowship is restored through forgiveness; refusal to forgive and reconcile with each other is a sin that bars us from receiving God's forgiveness. Refusing to forgive violates and ignores God's claim that vengeance belongs to Him alone.

## Train Your Children

Some years ago, David, a young man in his twenties, met Suzie, an attractive young girl in her teens. They began dating and few years later were married. David's parents had divorced when he was seven years old, and he had grown up without the guiding influence of a father. Now, as a husband, he did not know how to show his wife the love he felt for her. Two years after their wedding, Suzie announced they would be having a son. In David's new role as a father, he had no model to follow. He did not know how to relate to the boy who would soon look up to him for guidance and direction. David's situation is by no means unique. In a traditional, two-parent home, a young boy learns from his father how to be a man and how to show a proper love, care, and respect for his wife. From his mother, he learns about the behaviours of women and how they should be treated. Over time, he will transfer what he has learned from his parents to the woman who becomes his wife. Likewise, a young girl learns from her mother how to be a woman and cultivate the virtues that will make her a good wife and mother. And from her father, she learns what men are like and how a woman can support a man.

Parents, therefore, are the single most important influence on the way their son or daughter will raise his or her children. The home they establish should provide a climate conducive to the moral, spiritual, intellectual, and physical development of those who become a part of the family circle. Only by means of strong, godly values in the home can we develop a strong child and counteract the secular, materialistic, and immoral values of present-day society. But how can parents build this sort of home regardless of the problems facing them? Let us turn to the refreshing example of Enoch for encouragement and guidance in this matter.

Enoch faced many challenges and tensions similar to the type we're facing today. In many respects, his example can provide us with solutions to our problems. As we examine the scriptures, we find that it is not sufficient for us to give our children comfortable homes to live in or to give them toys, books, and sports equipment to play with. We must give of ourselves in constructive ways; as we do so, our children will learn to give of themselves. The happiness they derive from these values will, in turn, establish godly values in their lives.

## Opposing Values

Following Adam and Eve's expulsion from the garden of Eden and the murder of Abel, two separate traditions began to develop. These traditions were headed by Cain and Seth. Cain and his descendants were godless, whereas those in Seth's line retained some semblance of godliness as cities and civilisations began to thrive.

The irreligious character of the society in which Enoch and his family lived may be gleaned from two important facts. First, during this time, those descended from Seth began to call on the Lord in prayer (Gen. 4: 26); secondly, Enoch began to walk with the Lord. (Gen. 5: 24). The book of Hebrew 11:5 places the emphasis for this on God This is both qualitative and comparative. It points to the genuine nature of Enoch's experience and, at the same time, contrasts his encounter with the religious observance of those around him. Further confirmation of the irreligious character of Enoch's contemporaries may be found from other portions of the scriptures.

The psalmist touches on the way Enoch's contemporaries flagrantly rejected God's grace. He quotes them as saying, "God has forgotten, He hides His face from our sin, He will never see it" (Ps. 10: 11). The psalmist says further, "How does God know of our sin? Is there knowledge with the Most High?" (Ps. 73: 11). Even Eliphaz refers to the blasphemy of men in the days of Enoch. He asks Job, "Will you keep the old way which wicked men have trodden, who were snatched many before their time whose foundation was poured out as a stream? Who can say to God depart from us; and what can the Almighty do for them (i.e., the godly)?" (Job 22: 14–17). The men of Enoch's time felt that they could sin with impunity; they thought that God could not see them. The prevailing attitude in our society today seems to be that we can break God's law, flout his moral standard, and get away with it. The Bible says, "The fool said in his heart, there is no God, they are corrupt, their deeds are vile; there is no one who does good" (Ps. 14: 1). Despite living in a society where his contemporaries rejected God's grace, Enoch led an upright life of a believer. You can do the same today so you are not like a fool (Ps14: 1).

## Pattern and Process

We learn from the Bible that for the first sixty-five years of his life, Enoch lived the same kind of life as the other descendants of Seth. Then, "When Enoch had lived 65 years, he became the father of Methuselah and after he became the father of Methuselah, Enoch walked with God 300 years and had other sons and daughters. Altogether, Enoch lived 365 years. Enoch walked with God, then he was no more because God took him away" (Gen. 5: 21–24).

Enoch was outwardly godly but subject to the same encroachments of evil and slow deterioration of moral values as in our present-day society. Then a baby boy was born into his home: "and Enoch walked with God after he beget Methuselah" (Gen. 5: 22). Enoch held his son in his arms and felt the tiny fingers run over his face and grasped his hair; he wanted the best for his son. He began to imagine how his son would grow up. He dreamed about the kind of profession this son would follow and the way in which he would take his place in the community. He had great ambition for Methuselah, and he was determined to do everything possible to help him achieve them. Enoch suddenly realised that his son would grow to manhood in a dreadful world. How would Methuselah cope with the unbridled pride and flagrant lawlessness of the Canaanites? These thoughts frightened Enoch. What could he do to protect Methuselah from such a wicked environment? Should he drop out of society and take his family to start a new community? Or should he rear his son as an introverted spiritualist? In groping for answers, Enoch finally realised that the best thing he could do was to set a good example for his son. He could show Methuselah that if he was to live in this world and remain free from its contaminating influences, he would have to be a man of principle. From that moment on, Enoch reordered his life so that his son would have a good example to follow.

## Creative Precedent

As parents, we have the privilege of raising our children during their most impressionable years. Many of the fundamental attitudes they develop and the way they will later respond to external stimuli are formulated during their early period of growth. We must provide godly examples at home and at church during these years. We fail our children if we do not develop proper values in our homes and lay a foundation for them to cultivate healthy relationships. No educational training or firm will be able to make up for our failure and their loss. Enoch's influence on his son was positive, while the wickedness and lawlessness of the society around them thrived. The example he set for Methuselah included counsel and direction. Enoch counselled him on what to avoid and directed his footsteps in the way he should go. The book of Proverbs says, "Train up a child in the way he should go and when he is old he will not depart from it" (Prov. 22: 6).

Enoch knew that without God, he was insufficient for the task of raising his son. He therefore began to walk with God, and as he did so, he was able to show Methuselah how to live. Enoch also renounced the errors of the time and warned the godless people that the Lord would judge them for their ungodly deeds "Enoch, the seventh from Adam, prophesied about them 'See, the Lord is coming with thousands and thousands of his holy ones to judge everyone and to convict all the ungodly of all the ungodly acts they have done in the ungodly way and all the harsh words the ungodly sinners have spoken against him'" (Jude 1: 14–15 NIV)

This kind of teaching is shunned today. Psychologists tell us that prohibitions will set limits on the development of our children and limit their growth. Unfortunately, these professionals interpret Biblical principles as a set of rules and accuse Christians who live according to them of being legalistic. In contrast to this, Jesus said, "Come to me all you who are labour and are heavy laden, and I will give you rest. Take my yoke upon you and learn from Me. For I am gentle and lowly in heart, and you will find rest for your souls. For my yoke is easy and my burden is light" (Matt. 11: 29–30). The Bible counsels further: "And you shall know the truth and the truth shall make you free" (John 8: 32). Psychologists and others who attempt to ignore biblical principles fail to realise that God, the source of all wisdom, gave definite counsel to the sons of Israel on what was off limits for them to do. He said, "You shall not make anything to be with me – gods of silver or gods of gold you shall not make for yourself" (Exod. 20: 23). Even the Lord Jesus Christ did not hesitate to warn his disciples of the hypocrisy of the Pharisees and the contaminating influence of Herod: "Then Jesus said to them, 'Take heed and beware of the leaven of the Pharisees and the Sadducees'" (Matt. 16: 6).

In raising our children, we need to remember that the bricks that build good character are laid one by one. Each parent must have his or her own plumb line. That is, parents draw principles from scriptural counsel, and they impart them to their children as ways by which to measure right from wrong. In building character, just as in architecture, the plumb line is of the utmost importance. If the walls are cracked, the doors and windows will not fit correctly and the roof may tumble in, making the house unfit for habitation, only to be torn down or abandoned. As Christian parents, it is our solemn responsibility to set an example of godliness for our children, as Enoch did. We need to nurture them in the principles of righteousness and in appreciation of the significance of the word of God they need in order to be diligent and faithful to the Lord. Modelling adherence to sound biblical doctrine, respect for others, and loyalty to their nation is also of paramount importance. The character they develop will not be the product of a set of rules but the result of a system of values that they have observed from their superiors.

A task like this may seem difficult considering the days in which we are living, but it is certainly not impossible when we allow God, the Good Shepherd, to lead our families. We can also keep the story of Enoch in mind as an example; he realised his insufficiency and practised the principle of righteousness in his own life, making it easy for Methuselah to follow in his footsteps. As Enoch walked with God, he found out that he could triumph over his environment. He fulfilled his responsibility in all areas of life, and his wife enjoyed a natural, loving relationship with him. His leadership in the home stemmed from his walk with the Most High God; this made it easy for his wife to respond to him. Other children were born to them who could tell of the influence Enoch had on the other members of the line of Seth.

True worship involves total surrender of our lives to God. At the same time, it is always easier to follow the dictates of the five senses than the discipline of the Holy Spirit. These conflicting truths in human hearts have been in existence from the earliest time to the present. The Apostle Paul points out "that in departing from God, people suppress the truth and prefer their wickedness to the knowledge of God. Therefore, He gave them over to the sinful desires of their hearts, to sexual impurity for the degrading of their bodies with one another, even as they did not see it fit to acknowledge God any longer. He gave them over to reprobate mind, to become filled with all sorts of unrighteousness, wickedness, greed, and malice so that not only were their lives characterised by all kinds of evil, but they did not hesitate to give their hearty approval to those who practised the same vices" (Rom. 1: 24–32). Enoch walked with God in a similar environment and succeeded. Most of the moral practices in the West have made it nearly impossible for parents to train their children and enforce discipline at home. Beloved in Christ, you can do it if you invite God to shepherd your marriage and family. Whatever you commit into the hand of God comes out pure and perfect and becomes a living testimony for the world.

The psalmist writes, "The Lord is my shepherd I shall not be in want, he make me lie down in green pastures, he lead me besides quiet waters, he restored my soul. He guide me in the path of righteousness for His name sake" (Ps. 23: 1–3). Why not entrust the rulership of your marriage and family to God and let Him lead your family beside still waters and restore your soul to give you extraordinary testimonies?

### Household Rules

Even though only a few children would admit that they enjoy following rules, they all appreciate the structure that rules provide. This structure helps children feel safe and secure. In addition, rules provide expectations to help them understand and practise acceptable behaviours. Without rules, children live in a state of chaos and disorder which typically invites conflict and behavioural problems. In addition, where there are no rules, unfortunately, children learn to take matters into their own hands instead of informing their parents of the misbehaviour of others. This can lead to dire consequences. Behaviours such as violence, stealing, and lying thrive in environments without rules. There is a right and wrong way to establish household rules. I recommend the following effective principles for parents to follow when establishing household rules:

1. You should involve your children when creating household rules, because children are more apt to follow rules when their input is included.

2. The older your child is, the more rules you will need. For example, a toddler rule would be age-appropriate and specifically entitled something like "Do as you are told." As your child grows older, you could include additional rules to meet his or her growing needs.

3. If your child has difficulty reading, it would be appropriate for you to draw a picture next to each rule to help him or her identify it.

4. Do not create rules that cover every aspect of your child's life; only create rules that address specific behaviour he or she is having difficulty with. For instance, if your child always tells the truth, it might not be necessary to include this as a rule. Keep in mind that the more rules you have, the more difficulty you will have enforcing them.

5. When establishing rules for an older child, attempt to create fewer rules that are general enough to encompass several smaller rules within the same category. For example, a rule entitled "Keep your hands and feet to yourself" should include all inappropriate body contact such as hitting, kicking, tripping, and shoving others.

6. Make all rules sound positive rather than negative. Positive rules help children learn the behaviours they could engage in rather than focusing on the behaviour that they should not engage in.

7. Every rule needs to be clear, concise, and measurable so that everyone knows when a rule is broken. Rules must be specific to a particular behaviour rather than ambiguous. An example of this is a rule titled "respect others". Although this might sound appropriate, the word 'respect' is ambiguous and should be broken down to subcategories, defining the specific behaviours that are expected.

8. Rules can be updated at any time to meet new behaviours; for instance, a toddler would not require curfew rules but an adolescent would. It is important that you include your child's input when adding or updating household rules, just as it is when initially creating them.

### Communication

Communication is a vital tool in marriage. If a couple doesn't know how to communicate effectively with each other, marriage may be harder or difficult to enjoy. It is like having gold in the garden but not knowing how to dig it out. The gold is there, but you cannot be enriched by it until it is dug up. The basis of any fruitful and lasting relationship is effective communication. God proved His love for humans by communicating His plans and intentions to us through His prophets and other writers. He spoke clearly to Moses, Samuel, David and Isaiah, continuing through to Jesus Christ and those who loved him.

A marriage without effective communication does not work. A wise proverb says: "If you talk together, you stay together." God made marriage as an avenue for both husband and wife to find fulfilment through effective communication. Therefore, it becomes important for couples to understand the necessary tools of communication and apply them in their day-to-day relationship.

## What Is Communication?

Communication could be defined as the art of passing news, information, feelings, and so forth to somebody else, and vice versa. Communicating in words is considered verbal communication. There is also non-verbal communication, which includes facial expressions, body language, written communication, and so forth. Working from the provided definition, until you successfully pass a message or idea to someone else, you cannot be said to have communicated effectively. Communication therefore is a two-way process, involving talking and listening or comprehending each other.

There are two levels of communication, horizontal and vertical. On the horizontal level, it is between humans; for example, between husband and wife. On the vertical level, it is between humans and God. Therefore, effective communication with God makes communication between humankind more productive. Effective communication in marriage involves more than merely passing across a feeling, thought, message, or desire. It also involves the use of words and the proper medium to communicate an idea. Let's analyse the word even further. The long word "communication" is broken down to "communion", which means sharing of thoughts and feelings. Breaking the word down further, the word "commune" is found. To commune means to speak as close friends, and this makes oneness possible in marriage.

The more we work on effective communication within the family, the better we become at it. Every time there is a breakdown in communication, frustration follows; this leads to assumption, suspicion, and brutality. Adam and Eve were the perfect couple in their perfect world, but they missed something when it came to communication. Adam assumed that Eve understood the instruction of God. The devil knew that there was a breakdown in communication between the couple, and he took advantage of it, slipped in and beguiled Eve. "Did God truly say, you must not eat from any tree in the garden?" (Gen. 3: 1–2).

It is mandatory that Christian families adopt what I refer to as a "four-square" communication system in the family, with proper communication taking place between God, the husband, the wife, and the children.

Men who are too busy to spend quality time with their families are courting trouble. When God gives the wife or the husband a vision or assignment, the person who receives it needs to share it with his or her spouse and involve God, through prayer, explaining it gently until it is clearly understood. The husband, wife, and children should each have deep understanding of their place in their respective visions, especially when it is necessary to make a sacrifice. Therefore, all Christian spouses must learn to talk with each other, respect each other's views, and answer their children's questions.

## Components of Communication

There are certain things that make up effective communication in marriage. It will be of great benefit to look at them one by one so that cordial relationships can be established among family members for the husband and wife to experience overflowing love, joy, and happiness.

## Trust

Communicating in marriage and the larger family is a continuous process. It is important to communicate openly at all times. This is why trust is the number-one component in a family communication system.

You cannot effectively disclose your innermost dreams, desires, and thoughts to someone you don't trust. Trust forms an umbrella of confidence, faith, assurance, and reliability. One of men's major concerns about intimacy with women arises because women perceive information differently than men, and they may share in public what men see as personal, confidential matters. However, trust is essential if a couple is going to be able to communicate effectively. Women need to learn to be dependable. Family communication entails maintaining an attitude of openness – hiding nothing from each other. A man and his wife must work together by maintaining trust and confidentiality in all family matters; trust is the solid foundation for communication.

The promises we make to each other contribute to the trust we have for each other. Just as babies count on their mothers to be there when they need them, so also a wife counts on her husband to be there for her; likewise, the husband will count on the wife to be there whenever she is needed. When couples make promises during their communication, these commitments bind them together in trust; failure to deliver on these promises amounts to disloyalty and betrayal. Peter displayed disloyalty to our Lord Jesus when he denied that he knew him. Judas betrayed Jesus when he sold him to his enemies for thirty pieces of silver. A couple who goes about sharing their family dreams and aspirations with others betrays their marriage bond and trust. A wife who belittles her husband in public commits brutality and treason against him, and vice versa.

## Understanding

"Through wisdom is a house built and by understanding it is established" (Prov. 24: 3). That is, wisdom and understanding are the basis for effective communication in a home. Understanding enables you to read between the lines, interpret eye movements, body language and tone of voice, and it helps soften the harshness associated with anger.

When your spouse speaks, his or her words may be few, but because you understand your partner very well, he or she successfully communicates. In the Bible, Abigail was described as a woman with a good understanding; she understood the thirst for vengeance in David as she came against her ill-mannered husband and effectively communicated with him (1 Sam. 25: 23–35).

Many homes have been destroyed for lack of understanding; the husband misunderstands his wife, and the wife misreads meanings into her husband's actions and statements. But the word of God says: "good understanding giveth favour" (Prov. 13: 15). Frequent communication builds up trust and gives understanding. These are vital instruments for building a Christian family.

## Openness

"Hide not thyself from thine own flesh" (Isa. 58: 7). When a man takes a woman as a wife, the Bible says that in God's eyes, they are one flesh. In Ephesians 5: 28, God declares: "he that loves his wife loves himself". Therefore, a unique fusion occurs during marriage, a merging of two separate individuals into one. God expects that when two become one in holy wedlock, nothing should be kept secret between them. They must both be open to one another and walk in sincerity with one another. When wounds are hidden, they tend to fester and worsen, but when they are opened, healing begins to take place. Whatever is covered will eventually be exposed. But, as a unit, couples must learn to keep their secrets to themselves. Remember the experience of Joseph? He shared his dream with his parents and siblings and was sold into slavery for divulging it. When a family vision is shared with a third party, disaster could be just around the corner. Remember, three are not joined together in the marriage. Keep family secrets within the family to avoid satanic encroachment and manipulation.

## Vehicles for Effective Communication

When a person has goods to transport, he or she looks for a medium of transportation. The person considers the size of the goods and looks for an appropriate vehicle. Communication is like the goods; the person wanting to communicate searches for appropriate vehicles. The vehicles for effective communication are words expressed uprightly. Two people can say the same thing in different ways. While one person may successfully pass the message across, the other may not. Words can hurt or heal, and couples must learn to express upright and effective words in their daily communication with each other as described in the Bible: "A word fully spoken is like apples of gold in pictures of silver" (Prov. 25: 11).

Choosing the appropriate words is a must for husbands and wives; it is an art that must be learnt. One's choice of words must be so immersed in love that it conveys the message without being disrespectful to one's spouse or trampling upon his or her feelings. A woman will respond to the intent of proper words by speaking in a way that boosts her husband's ego. Paul writes, "Let no corrupt communication proceed out of your mouth, but that which is good to the use of edifying that it may minister grace unto the hearers" (Eph. 4: 29). Similarly, the writer of Proverbs says, "From the fruit of his lips a man is filled with good things as surely as the work of his hands rewards him" (Prov. 12: 15 NIV).

These scriptural truths certainly comes from the heart of God regarding negative communication between couples. Negative communication proceeds from the mouth, but it has roots in the heart. When everything you think about your spouse is negative and you focus only on his or her deficiencies, eventually you will only speak negative things. "For out of the abundance of the heart the mouth speaks" (Prov. 23: 7). The Bible also says, "Do not let any unwholesome talk come out of your mouths, but only what is helpful for building others up according to their needs, that it may benefit those who listen" (Eph. 4: 29).

Communication in Christian marriages and families is most effective when family members are united together in praying, praising, worshipping, and sharing the word of God. This establishes the family as an extension of the kingdom of God.

## Family Relationships

Every stable building has a foundation, and every river has a source. People drink water but rarely think of appreciating its source. Any family without peaceful and cordial relationships has an unstable foundation not built upon Jesus Christ.

God said in His word: "And if a kingdom be divided against itself, that kingdom cannot stand, and if a house be divided against itself, that house cannot stand" (Mark 3: 24–25).

Let's expand upon this excerpt from the book of Mark to better our understanding. A family home is a smaller kingdom within the kingdom of God. If the family home is unstable, that implies that its foundation was laid on ground that has no strength rather than on solid rock. Matthew 7: 6 says, "Give not that which is holy unto the dogs. Neither cast ye your pearls before swine, lest they trample then under their feet and turn again and rend you." Many homes remain unsettled, scattered and chaotic, overshadowed with hatred and bitterness because they have defiled God's plan for moral marriages. The Bible outlines the timeless principles of marriage that provide a guide for a successful home. Jesus will forever be the foundation of any marriage that desires to be secure. Some homes have taken worldly morals as their guide. Some have buried good morality, which leads to degeneration of good behaviour. Even modernisation in the Western world has resulted in immorality and indecent behaviour in many homes. Such families have allowed Satan to destroy what they have built.

A home that is not formed on the fundamental truth of Jesus Christ will collapse.

The word of God states the roles of a father, mother, and children in the family as follows: "For the husband is the head of the wife, even as Christ is the head of the Church, and he is the Saviour of the body. Therefore, as the Church is subject unto Christ, so let the wife be to their husbands in everything. Husbands love your wives even as Christ also loved the Church and gave himself for it" (Eph. 5: 23–25). It also says, "Children, obey your parents in all things; for this is well pleasing unto the Lord. Fathers, provoke not your children to anger, lest they be discouraged" (Col. 3: 20–21).

This presentation of the hierarchical structure of the family says that the man is the head of the family and has authority that surpasses that of the wife. But how is the husband using his authority?

The husband's authority over his wife, as directed by God, is not dictatorial, like the master and slave relationship; the husband must not see his wife as property. The Lord gives husbands an authority like that of the Good Shepherd.

My research on marriage and family life has shown that relationships in some homes are not far from the level of merciless hatred because the head of the family either doesn't see himself as such or takes undue authority over his home, thereby creating fears in the hearts of his family members. This illustrates that if the centre cannot hold, things will definitely fall apart.

The husband must not abdicate his authority as the head of the family to his wife under any circumstances or situation, lest the family relationship degenerate to chaos. This will tear the cord that binds the family together. If a man does give up his authority, it is commonly because he has low self-esteem or feels insufficient somehow. In this situation, the wife would be more self-confident than her husband. The man becomes the "wife", and the wife becomes the "husband", creating abnormalities in the institution of marriage. If a man exerts undue authority, it may be as a result of his being born in a higher economic, social, or political status. He treats everyone in his domain as slaves and subjects them to his will at all times, thereby upsetting the cordial relationships that are supposed to be in a family. This philosophy of life affects the children leads to their views of being disregarded. Children from such a family will be less likely to lead interesting, fruitful lives "Every wise woman buildeth her house; but the foolish plucketh it down with her hand" (Prov. 14: 1 KJV).

The responsibility of holding the centre in a family together falls on the wife. She must have an exemplary character of dignity, respect, love, fear of God, affection, meekness, motherliness, and many more virtues. This will build up her children and stabilize the home and bring about good relationships within the family. Women should not go beyond their authority but rather hold on to the truth. They should maintain peace in the family and keep the husband on check.

## Finances and Marriage

Financial management between a husband and wife is a big issue in every family, and it needs to be addressed at least briefly in this book, although there is not enough room here for a complete discussion.

The Bible says: "Two are better than one, because they have a good return for their work: If one falls down, his friend can help him up. But pity the man who falls and has no one to help him up. Also, if two lie down together, they will keep warm. But how can one keep warm alone? Though one may be overpowered, two can defend themselves. A cord of three strands is not quickly broken" (Eccl. 4: 9–12)

Pooling strength, resources, and wisdom together seems overwhelming when one is single or alone, but this usually changes when one finds a spouse and forms a successful marriage. Financial management between husbands and wives demands total adherence to Christian marriage principles such as love, truth, forgiveness, trustworthiness, openness, mutuality, honour, and respect for each other. It also requires the implementation of the principle of a one-flesh union to establish common family vision and destiny to bring about a clear sense of direction for the family. This will enable a couples to commit their resources to common family projects.

# Chapter Five

# FAMILY STRUCTURES
# AND ETHICAL VALUES

The Kingdom of God is based upon relationship, and the central relationship of the kingdom is one of parent to child, father and mother to sons and daughters. This is the fundamental structure and values in marriage and family; husband, wife and children must be a reflection of the nature of God in their relationship.

Naturally, all other creatures like animals, birds, fishes and all crawling species procreates without marriage and family system. But because of the uniqueness in marriage and nuclear family system which only existed among humanity, the Bible expressly laid the divine structure of marriage and family thus: But I would have you know, that the head of every man is Christ, and the head o the woman is the man, and the head of Christ is God. (1 Corinthians 11:3)

God is the giver of life, the journey of life began from God through His word and His Spirit from whom life flow into man and man became a living soul. (Genesis 2:7), Bible recorded that "In the beginning was the word and the word was with God and the word was God. The same was in the beginning with God. All things were made by him; and without him was not any thing made that was made. In him was life and the life was the light of men. (John 1:1-4)

The above bible passages confirmed that creation including human are products of the word of God, and the word is the final authority over all creation while the Spirit of God quickened and sustain all things and the souls of men deep-rooted in Him. All things were made by Him, and without him was not anything made that was made. (John 1;5)

Since God was the life giver and His Spirit sustains all creations, it is also worth knowing that the word of God is the constitution of life that must be obeyed by all created beings including the angels, man and all creatures, otherwise, life will turn chaotic and negative, hence the need to carefully studied and abide by the rules that established the institution of marriage and family.

God established marriage institution and saddled the couples with responsibilities to govern the earth (Genesis 1:26-28) The structure of marriage and family is therefore sacred and the sanctity must be uphold.

As previously mentioned, marriage and family was God's initiative, He established it purposely for man who was created in the image and likeness of God with the mandate to rule and be blessed for the glory of God.

Marriage was a platform upon which God releases dominion power to mam to govern the earth with the blessing to be fruitful, multiply and subdue the earth (Genesis 1:28) Marriage is a spiritual and sacred institution that must be taught and understood by all human who truly want to succeed in their marriage and family life for the glory of God.

Marriage is the ultimate expression of God's love towards man, its transcend human culture, tradition, religion and modern civilisation that we are familiar with today, marriage was the first government and the first Church on earth, and God is the arrow head of both..

## GODLY FAMILY ORDER

Marriage was the crown over the works of creation of the earth, and the ultimate expression of God's love for humanity. It is a sacred institution where both husbands and wives are meant to manifest the nature of God, exercising honour and respect to nurture each other's life within the beautiful marriage estate and raising their children in line with God commandments to establish godly societies and to secure everlasting generational blessings.

God desires that every husbands should represent his image and likeness as it was from the beginning, just as God the Father, Son and Holy Spirit are ONE indivisible, so husband and wife ought be.one flesh, soul and spirit.

**Jesus is the head of the man:** as narrated in the Bible: and the word was made flesh and dwell among us (and we beheld his glory, the glory as of the only begotten of the Father) full of grace and truth (John 1:14)

Above bible passage clearly states that Jesus is the word personified, spoken by God to create all things including human and the marriage institution, he therefore must be the head of every man who desire to be a successful husband and rule over his wife in alignment with how Jesus relate with His Father in heaven… for I came down from heaven, not to do my own will but the will of him that sent me.

Since the creation of woman and the establishment of marriage was the will and the expression of God's love, it places a sacred demand on the man "husband" to love his wife even as Jesus loved His Church and gave himself for it (Ephesians 5:25) and uphold the sanctity of the marriage as the true likeness of God. The man must husband his wife with the word and fear of God ultimately, without which, man cannot do anything successfully in marriage (John 5:5)

**The man is the head of the wife:** This is a sacred responsibility of husbands toward their wives. Husbands, love your wives even as Christ also loved the Church, and gave himself for it; that he might sanctify and cleanse it with the washing of water by the word. That he might present it to himself a glorious Church, not having spot, or wrinkle, or any such thing; but that it should be holy and without blemish. So ought men to love their wives as their own bodies, he that love his wife loves himself. (Ephesians 5:25-28).

**It is a great and incomparable responsibility for man to love his own wife unconditionally,** in same manner that God the Father loved the world and gave his only begotten Son (John 3:16) and the Son loved man (friends) and gave himself up as a living sacrifice to redeem man. (John 15:13) so also a husband ought to love his wife. No women hate to be loved. This is the life-wire that connected husbands to the trinity Godhead.

Let me add values to the issue of love and why every husband must love **"agape"** his wife, Love flows from God because God is Love Himself, and creation is an act of the love of God. A man who cannot love his wife passionately and tenderly does not know God.

When true and genuine love is expressed by a husband who is the head toward his wife, a reaction that will activate submissiveness will follow, unless if the woman is possess of evil spirits like pride, arrogant and domineering spirit.

Every husbands ought to regard their wives as a mother, I learned this in my marriage, realising how every babies often draw near to their mother to feed from their breast, I also took pleasure in this act with my wife and she joyfully obliged... similarly, we are the best of friends, brother and sister, these are the values that should fuel every love relationship between husbands and wives, cultured in the act of honour and respect for each other. Every marriage must be romantic to establish deeper affection.

**HUSBANDS, NURTURE YOUR WIVES WITH LOVE, SHE'S YOUR QUEEN. THERE'S WISDOM IN DOING SO; IT PROMOTES GOOD HEALTH, LONGEVITY, PEACE, SUCCESS AND BLESSINGS.**

**Wives responsibilities towards their husbands:** Wives, submit unto your husbands, as unto the Lord; for the husband is the head of the wife, even as Christ is the head of the Church and he is the saviour of the body. Therefore as the church is subject unto Christ, so let the wives be to their own husbands in everything. (Ephesians 5:24)

The above passages revealed the spiral effect between the Triune God, the marriage institution and the Church of God headed by

Christ. a divine narration of how God is directly involved and should rule every marriages and families. Both men and women in marriages has a significant role to play to ensure that the will of God is established on earth.

To be a woman re-enforces perfect creation, but wife is a title of a woman who represent the Church and joined in holy wedlock with a man in marriage; she must submits to her husband in reference to the Lord. It is a divine instruction for wives to submit to their husband **'why' because every wife was a bone drawn out of her husband ribs** (Genesis 2:21-22) so the man is the crown and king over the wife irrespective of their status in life, this is divine order that is beyond every human logical reasoning, a concept that enhances respect and honour amongst godly family, a platform for perfect role model for the children to build a godly society, and the ultimate desire of God when he established marriage as a crowning works of creation..

The concept of godly marriage is the one that operate within the dimension of God's love, truth, forgiveness, caring, respect and honour for each other and ultimately live to praise, worship, and honour God almighty the Creator.

No wonder, Sarah recognises this divine rules in her marriage and she addresses her husband as **'my lord'** Bible recorded that: like Sarah who obeyed Abraham and called him her lord. You are her daughters if you do what is right and do not give way to fear. (1 Peter 3:6). When a wife submit to her husband, she has ultimately submitted to God and His Christ.

**Children responsibility towards their parents:** Honour thy father and they mother that thy days may be long upon the land which the Lord thy God giveth thee. (Exodus 20:12)

The life journey of every child started from God through their fathers and mothers, every child were first incubated in their father's incubators and later incubated in the womb of their mothers before they are birthed on earth, this is the process for a life journey of every child.

Since every human are the product of the word of God, God's sovereign authority over our lives is supreme and final, any attempt to violate such rules could be very catastrophic. Bible says: honour thy father and thy mother as the Lord thy God hath commanded thee; that thy days may be prolonged, and that it may go well with thee, in the land which the Lord thy God giveth thee. (Deuteronomy 5:16

Above bible text anchored the lives of every children born into this world, either they believe or not, God, the giver of life have made it compulsory for every child to honour, respect and obey their parents to allow for the full manifestation of the blessing of God in their lives and all things in divine alignment to the will of God.

Let's examine how life and blessing flows from God down the line to father, mother and children. Bible recorded that "in the beginning, God created the heaven and the earth, and the earth was void and the Spirit of God was hovering

## THE FLOW OF LIFE

God created (Genesis 1:1) with His Word (John 1:3), and God breathed His Spirit into human nostrils, and man became a living soul (Genesis 2:7). Then God articulated that it is not good for a man to be alone (Genesis 2:18). He created the help meet with a bone he removed from the rib of Adam and presented Eve to Adam as a wife (Genesis 2:21-22), and Adam celebrated the gift of a wife (Genesis 2:23), then God contracted the marriage (Genesis 2:24) and blessed them (the couple)."God said unto them, Be fruitful, and multiply, and replenish the Earth, and subude it and have dominion over the fish of the sea, and over the fowl of the air, and over every living thing that moveth upon the Earth." (Genesis 1:28)

Above narration about the flow of life from God to man places a compulsory demand on humanity to obey the supreme instruction of God over life particularly within the marriage institution and family life.

Humanity are uniquely and wonderfully created and designed to manifest the nature of God as the product of the word and bearer of the Spirit of God to enjoy perfect relationship and fellowship with God without blemish. Worship should therefore flow from the heart of the husband to God to generate agape love toward the wife who is the life wire and governor of the house. The wife must also reciprocate with honour and submissiveness to her husband, this is the template upon which the children who are the fruit of the marriage learn mutual respect, honour and obedience to their parents as commanded by God.

**Parent's godly responsibilities towards their children:** He that spareth his rod hateth his son: but he that loveth him chasterneth him betimes (Prov. 13:24) a great responsibility is placed in the hands of the parents to ensure discipline, obedience, moral values and fear of God among the children.

Parents are blessed with children as treasures for catering, discipline and training in the way of the Lord. Parents are to guide their children in the way of truth and righteousness, to love God with all their myth, to love their neighbours, communities and nations like themselves (Matthew 22:37-39)

It is also important for parents to teach their children moral, spiritual and family values, so they may be useful to themselves, their parents, and the society they belong and to God almighty. Bible says: You shall teach them to your sons, talking of them when you sit in your house, and when you walk along the road and when you lie down and when you rise up. (Deuteronomy 11:19)

The greatest strength in raising children by every parents are in their ability to bring their marriage in alignment with the will of God and treating them with love. Bible says: Fathers, do not provoke your children to anger, but bring them up in the discipline and instruction of the Lord. (Ephesians 6:4) Tell your sons about it, and let sons tell their sons, and their sons the next generation. (Joel 1:3)

Every parents has spiritual responsibility to pray and prophesy into the lives of their children everyday till the end, no parent should curse their children whatever the situation could be. Bible says: He blessed Joseph, and said, The God before whom my fathers Abraham, and Isaac walked, the God who has been my shepherd all my life to this day. The Angel which redeemed me from all evil, bless the lads; and let my name be named on them, and the name of my fathers Abraham and Isaac and let them grow into a multitude in the midst of the earth. (Genesis 48:15-16)

**Examples of parental blessings for children.** The book of Genesis emphacises the blessing of a father to his sons.the patriarchs, Abraham, Isaac and Jacob all gave formal blessings to their children, and in Jacob case to some of his grandchildren.

An Old Testament blessing of a father to his sons included words of encouragement regarding inheritance and prophetic words concerning their future. For example, Isaac's blessing for Jacob which was meant for Isau gave Jacob earthly bounty and authority over his elder brother Esua (Genesis 27:28-29) It also includes that those who will bless Jacob shall be blessed. And those who curse Jacob would be cursed, echoing God's covenant with Abraham in (Genesis 12:3)

Similarly, when Jacob blessed his twelve sons, he also made predictions regarding their future (Genesis 49) Bible contains records of the fulfilment of Jacob's blessings of his sons, for example, Jacob blessed Judah and said: Judah, thou art he whom thy brethren shall praise: thy hand shall be in the neck of thine enemies; thy father's children shall bow before thee.(Genesis 49:8) Jacob's blessing for Judah also include the prediction that kings would come from Judah and that one king would eventually receive the 'obedience of the nations' verse 10. Judah descendants later became the tribe from which King David came and in whose land Jerusalem was located and Jesus Christ also came from the tribe of Judah. (Matthew 1:3)

Parents, fathers and mothers, there is the power of life and dead in your tongues (Proverbs 18:21) use your tongues to bless your children and prophesy the blessing of God into their future. This are the Godly family values and the cord of association that was founded by God from the beginning, hence the bible recorded the following structures: *But I would have you know that the head of every man is Christ, and the head of the woman is the man; and the head of Christ is God. (1 Corinthians 11:3)*

The best way to look at this is when God created us, He built into us a cavity where He Himself would fit into our lives (Genesis 1:26) we were created so we would never be complete without God our creator, and by extension we would then enter into marriage and raises fruits in the image and likeness of God. This need to be alive in every godly marriage and family homes in order to live for a purpose greater than our own natural ability.

## PARENTAL LOVE AND DISCIPLINARY ACTIONS

Bible says: He who spares the rod hates his son, but he who loves him is careful to discipline him – Proverbs 13:24;

Without correction and discipline, parents will produce rebellion and unruly children who will in turn grow up to become menace in the society. Abandoned, unloved, uncared and indiscipline children are the categories of youths who engaged in various criminal and violence activities worldwide. God demand stern responsibility from the parents to put the children on check from infancy to youthful age. Bible says: The rod of correction imparts wisdom: but a child left to himself disgraces his mother. (Proverbs 29:15)

Being a father, I have come to a place of understanding that parental roles includes love and discipline for our children is very crucial, the wisdom saying of my people "Yoruba kingdom" where I was born says: "parents are to discipline their children with right hand and also express unconditional love with their left hands" to enforce corrective discipline. Psychologically, when parents love their children and care for them, they feel belonging and develop sense of direction, but lack of discipline and abandoning children to live in their own world is perilous, they may join wrong pair mates and freely developed negative life.

## Family Cord of Association

The cord of association in any family will continue to be put under stress and be strained if the following points are not addressed.

(a) If both parties (husband and wife) and one party sinned before marriage and has not repented of it, both should seek solace in God. "If we confess our sins, He is faithful and just to forgive us our sins and to cleanse us from all unrighteousness" (1 John 1: 9).

(b)  No matter how rich the family is, if the family members are not yet born again, they will never fully discover how to relate cordially in the family. They may subject their home to disarray, disorder, perfidiousness and above all, the wrath and annoyance of God.

(c)  There is no tribe under heaven that God did not endow with a culture that speaks volumes of morality, association, good character and so forth. Because many people adopt human philosophy, it has become increasingly difficult to distinguish what the dos and don'ts of a culture are, resulting in the adulteration of ideals. For example, in Yoruba kingdom in Nigeria, where I came from, a man prostrates and a woman kneels anytime they want to greet their parents. What we have today in Yoruba kingdom is a borrowed culture, where neither the children nor the parents observe those cultural norms because of the indiscipline which we call modernisation. Children refuse to relate to their parents or follow these traditions anymore as they grow up.

(d)  Lack of parental care make many children hate their parents because they were denied this proper care when due. Are you a parent who feels on top of the world at the expense of your children? You can't expect to receive the best of relationships with them! It is very important for parents to manage the moral behaviour of their children so that they grow up well. Such children will appreciate this teaching all their lives since it moulds good character in them.

# Chapter Six

# THE ULTIMATE REWARD
# FOR A FAITHFUL FAMILY

### What to Know

Relationship in a family involves more than bearing the same name. Godly family relationships demonstrate love, affection, care, tolerance, liberty, faithfulness, moral uprightness, forgiveness, and the fear of God. If for any reason the above characteristics are not reflected in your family, heed the alarm bell of potential doom unless the situation is reversed. There can never be relationships other than treachery and confusion. The Bible says: "And Jesus knows their thoughts and said unto them, every kingdom divided against itself is brought to desolation; and every city or house divided against itself shall not stand" (Matt. 12: 25).

No matter how high a couple's education level or social status, the way they relate to each other speaks volumes. If their interactions expose egotism, imperiousness, insincerity, and hatred, such a family will be in darkness, and the seed of peace will not be planted in their home

## Parental Influence

Let us not be deceived; if the relationship between a father and mother is not cordial, then the chances of failure in the relationship between the children in the home and their parents is very high. Psychologically, there is a tendency for girls, especially those who are closer to their fathers, to grow up looking for the same characteristics in their husbands as in their father. Similarly, little boys grow up looking for their mother's traits in their wives. This shows us to what extent our parents shape our lives. This also explains why a man or woman who has undergone a traumatic childhood as a result of his or her parents losing a cordial relationship finds it difficult to adjust to real-life experiences. Their views, instincts, emotions, sense of good judgement, and idea of good relationships in a family have been shaped by the only family environment they knew. Our experiences as children, to a large extent, are what shape us into what we are today. Because of this, the way parents demonstrate marriage and family relationships in the home should not subject their children to a world of apprehensiveness in their quest to define life.

Children should also understand their primary responsibilities towards their parents. Paul writes, "Children, obey your parents in the Lord, for this is right. Honour your father and mother which is the first commandment with a promise, that it may go well with you and that you may enjoy long life on the earth" (Eph. 3: 1–3).

Parents should live an exemplary life and inculcate their children's minds from a young age with the desire and ambition to become leaders of nations as they prepare them for an excellent life.

Obeying and honouring our parents is the key to an excellent and successful life. It is a divine system put in place by God to release wisdom, knowledge, and understanding that will nurture children's growth to a higher level of leadership.

## Restitution in Marriage

When you do something to hurt a loved one, often there is a strong desire to do something good to make up for the wrong or to make the bad feelings go away. These are called acts of restitution, which people do to demonstrate feelings of remorsefulness and to reduce the distress of the injured partner. Restitution is an attempt by the offending partner to balance the scales by doing meaningful and important positive things for the offended partner.

As the one who caused the injury, you need to examine the extent to which making amends is important for you to move forward. It is important to recognize that moving past all the traumas in your marriage will probably occur eventually when you actively work at caring for your partner's distress, and nurturing your relationship is important even if the injured partner does not seem to acknowledge these efforts or does not respond in a positive way. You may have to persist in your efforts to make restitution before things improve.

For the spouse who was harmed, it is difficult to move beyond deep hurts unless he or she is assured that the person who caused such harm has committed not to cause hurt in that way again. Efforts towards reform by the partner who caused hurt include three steps.

1. Pledging never to hurt your partner in the same way again.

2. Addressing conditions that contributed to the issue.
3. Acting differently when confronted with similar situations in the future.

It is not realistic for partners to promise never to hurt one another in any form. But it is realistic to commit to avoiding certain hurtful behaviours – such as keeping secrets or engaging in inappropriate sexually or emotionally intimate relationships outside the marriage.

## The Complete Marriage and Family

The journey of every marriage relationship that is intended to be a lifelong project, as established by God, must begin and end with the following four types of love: (1) agape, (2) phileo, (3) storge, and (4) eros. These kinds of love are highly essential, and they are all needed within families to make marriage relationships strong, solid, and complete.

The highest of these types of love is **agape** love; this is unconditional love that can keep loving someone when other types of love fail. Agape love originates from God into the heart of anyone who accepts Jesus Christ as their personal Lord and Saviour and is baptised in the Holy Spirit and fire. God is the origin and the perfect example of **agape** love. He demonstrated agape love towards us in that while we were still sinners, Christ died for us (Rom 5: 8). He commands husbands to love their wives as Christ also loved the Church and gave Himself for her (Eph. 5: 25).

Human love is sometimes based on surface values, but agape love goes beyond the surface and enables us to look into the hearts of our spouses and love them for who God has made them to be, despite their shortcomings.

**Phileo** love is an enjoyable type of love; it makes one have tender affection towards his or her spouse. **Phileo** love is the platform for starting and building friendships. Phileo love is generally referred to as human love or brotherly love. It's one thing to unconditionally love (agape) someone who you don't like if he or she is nearby. It's another thing to unconditionally love someone who is tenderly affectionate (phileo) toward you. God's desire for the husband and wife is that they tenderly love each other while they overlook each other's faults and failures.

The tender affection of phileo love makes the unconditional love of agape enjoyable. It is how we experience the joy of friendship in family life.

**Storge** is the third type of love needed in marriage. This type of love is the physical demonstration of affection from pure motives like hugging, kissing, or other genuine expressions of affection. Wives regularly need this type of love from their husbands to feel loved and appreciated. It is therefore very important for the husband to set aside a reasonable time of companionship to meet his wife's need for affection.

**Eros** love is the fourth type of love that makes a strong marriage. It is the fulfilment of the physical and sexual desires that the husband and wife show to each other to make their two bodies become one flesh (Matt. 19: 5).

When all four of these types of love operate in a marriage, the relationship will be solid and complete, showing a picture of a perfect one-flesh union, where the husband and wife lay down their lives for each other (agape love). No matter how many times they offend each other, they will always forgive each other, enjoy each other's company because of the phileo love; they will freely hug and kiss each other with affection because they are each other's best friend.

When the hearts of husbands and wives are filled with agape, phileo, and storge love, a warm and passionate desire will arise within both of them for sexual intimacy (eros). This type of marriage will weather any storm.

# IMPORTANT RULES FOR HUSBANDS AND WIVES

KEEP GOD FIRST

PRAY TOGETHER

UNDERSTAND THAT LOVE IS A CHOICE, NOT MERELY A FEELING

RESPECT & HONOUR EACH OTHER!

ENCOURAGE EACH OTHER TO GROW TOGETHER!

HAVE A "MISSION STATEMENT" FOR YOUR MARRIAGE & FAMILY

READ THE BIBLE TOGETHER AS MUCH AS POSSIBLE!

DO NOT LET OTHERS COME BETWEEN YOU & YOUR SPOUSE!

BE SWIFT TO HEAR & SLOW TO SPEAK!

PROTECT & HONOUR YOUR MARRIAGE VOW

TAKE TIME TO COMMUNICATE WITH EACH OTHER

### Divine Wedding Feast

Can the wedding guests fast while the bridegroom is at the wedding feast with them? "Now John's disciples and the Pharisees were fasting. Some people came and asked Jesus, How is it that John's disciples and the disciples of the Pharisees are fasting, but yours are not? Jesus answered, How can the guests of the bridegroom fast while he is with them? They cannot so long as they have him with them" (Mark 2: 18–19).

Here, Jesus uses a simple and evocative image. Christ is the bridegroom who announces his wedding feast, a feast of love between God and humanity. He is the bridegroom who wants to communicate His joy to His guests. The bridegroom's friends are the believers, the obedient followers, who are invited to share in the inexhaustible glory, riches, blessing, and prosperity at the entrance into eternity for humankind. The wedding feast is the entrance into the fullness of the revelation of Jesus Christ our Lord and the consummation of the institution of marriage.

This feast is the result of Christ's inevitable conflict with, and victory over, the power of evil in order to bring about His presence, Emmanuel. "The light shines in the midst of the darkness, and the darkness has not overcome it" (John 1: 5).

The forgiven sins of all humanity play an essential part in this wedding feast. When Jesus died on the Crost and removed the veil that separated humankind from God, He restored the grace for believers to be in His presence at all times. But the failure of Jesus's own people to recognise this important values was particularly distressing for Christ. Addressing the city of Jerusalem as he approached her, He said, "You did not know the time of your visitation (Luke 19: 44).

There were those who gave a positive response, the response of faith, to Christ's presence on earth. Luke describes Jesus's royal, messianic entry into Jerusalem: "When the whole multitude of the disciples began to rejoice and praise God with a loud voice for all the mighty works that they had seen, saying: 'Blessed is the King who comes in the name of the Lord! Peace in heaven and glory in the highest'" (Luke 19: 37–39).

But this enthusiasm could not, in Jesus's eyes, disguise or outweigh His rejection by the leaders of His own people and the crowd they had incited. Moreover, before His triumphal entry into Jerusalem, Jesus foretold His sacrifice "For the Son of man also come not to be served but to serve, and to give his life as a ransom for many" (Mark 10: 45). The time of Christ's earthly life is thus marked by His redeeming sacrifice. The salvation of the human family flows from this paschal mystery of His death and resurrection.

> When the hour came, Jesus and his Apostles reclined at the table and He said to them, I have eagerly desired to eat this Passover with you before I suffer. For I tell you, I will not eat it again until it finds fulfilment in the kingdom of God. After taking the cup, he gave thanks and said, Take this and divide it among you. For I tell you I will not drink again of the fruit of the vine until the kingdom of God comes. And he took bread, gave thanks and broke it, and gave it to them, saying, "This is my body given for you; do this in remembrance of me".

> In the same way, after the supper he took the cup,
> saying. "This cup is the new covenant in my blood,
> which is poured out for you. (Luke 22: 14–20)

Jesus longed to partake of that final Passover with His disciples and anticipated the messianic banquet in the heavenly kingdom. He desires to be with you, and you with Him, always; hence, His promise to go and prepare a place for us believers in his Father's house and return to take us to be with him in his Father's kingdom (John 14: 1–6).

I strongly recommend that churches should offer teachings and seminars for both singles and married couples on the subject of marriage. These classes would create deeper awareness of the foundational values of life grounded in marriage and raising the standard of family values on earth. I also recommend churches conduct Holy Communion services to all married couples to remind them of their marriage vows. Couples must be encouraged to seal their marriage with the blood of the Lamb regularly with Holy Communion during their family prayer meetings.

## Back in the Garden of Eden

Perhaps you have taken a pleasant stroll through some botanical gardens or the grounds at holiday resorts, and you were impressed by the beauty and tranquillity. Now, let's compare these experiences with the garden in Eden and see how well the Lord provided for Adam and Eve. Every need they had was met. Let us also consider some of the features God put in place for the pleasure of the first couple on earth.

The garden was in Eden (Gen. 2: 8). It was not a legendary place or a dream in the mind of the writer of the book of creation. Certainly, the garden was on earth. In this story of creation, God is pictured as a gardener who prepared a large area of land as a place of refreshment and enjoyment for humanity. "The Lord God planted a Garden" (Gen. 2: 8), Our Lord Jesus Christ establishes the truth of the garden's existence when he says, "I am the True Vine, and my Father is the Gardener" (John 15: 1). Jesus describes Himself as the vine that sustains lives and His Father as the gardener who nurtures lives. Without the vine, the branches are useless and cannot bear fruit. Jesus goes further, saying, "I am the true vine, you are the branches. If a man remains in me and I in him, he will bear much fruit; apart from me you can do nothing" (John 15: 5).

Beloved people of God, God used this well-watered location to produce a garden with plenty of fruits and vegetation and to provide a purposeful occupation for the first couple. The God who prepared this wonderful and pleasing garden for the first human couple has prepared a similar garden for all his redeemed people. Jesus said, "I go to prepare a place for you" (John 14: 2).

God has not destroyed the garden but simply expelled the disobedient couple from it. I can assure you that our God, who created all things perfectly, is a loving God. His love is limitless, and He is forever willing to admit all obedient believers into the garden. "The Lord will surely comfort Zion and will look with compassion on all her ruins; he will make her deserts like Eden, her water lands like the Garden of the Lord" (Isa. 51: 3).

Husbands and wives, have you ever considered that your marriage is established in the garden of the Lord? As Matthew 18: 26 says,

"With God all things are possible" (NIV). If you will allow God to rule over your marriage and your family life, most assuredly I say unto you, your family will live in a state like the garden of Eden here on earth.

> Then I saw a new heaven and a new earth, for the first heaven and the first earth had passed away and there was no longer any sea. I saw the Holy City, the New Jerusalem, coming down out of heaven from God. Prepared as a bride beautifully dressed for her husband, and I heard a loud voice from the throne saying. Now the dwelling of God is with men, and he will live with them. They will be his people, and God himself will be with them and be their God. He will wipe every tear from their eyes. There will be no more death or mourning or crying or pain, for the old order of things has passed away. He who was seated on the throne said, I am making everything new! Then he said, write this down, for these words are trustworthy and true. (Rev. 21: 1–5) NIV

Husbands and wives, imagine if Satan had not come into the earth to deceive and distort the perfect lives of Adam and Eve. What would have happened to marriages and to our world? The state of the earth would have remained the same as it was in the garden of Eden: picturesque, comfortable, and peaceful without rancour. You can stand in the gap for your family, to break away from any negative tendencies and foundational errors in your generation. Pray for your marriage to follow the heart of God, and it shall be well with you forever. Let this be the collective vision of you and your spouse as you join together and journey through the storms of life. Jesus says: "And surely I'm with you always to the very end of the age" (Matt. 28: 20b).

There was plenty of water and plenty to eat in the garden of Eden. In fact, it is possible that the word "mist" (Gen. 2: 6) should be translated "flood" or "spring", which was the fountain producing a river which "went out of Eden to water the garden (Gen. 2: 10) to nurture the garden for the comfort of man". With such an abundance of water, every tree grew and bore much fruit that was so "pleasant to the sight and good for food" (Gen. 2: 9). God made it very clear to Adam and his wife, Eve, that there was no shortage of food when He said, "From every tree in the garden you may freely eat" (Gen. 2: 16). God is not a miser; He gives us abundantly all the things we need to enjoy life. "Command those who are rich in this present world not to be arrogant nor to put their hope in wealth, which is so uncertain, but to put their hope in God, who richly provides us with everything for our enjoyment" (1 Tim. 6: 17).

Jehovah is not a monotonous God, either; He created all that was pleasant and beautiful to look at with variety of colour and form. The garden of Eden was certainly a delightful place to live; that is why the name suggests pleasure and delight. The garden was vibrant with life; there was the life-giving running water, representing Jesus as the water of life, and an abundance of vegetation. In addition, "The tree of life was also in the midst of the garden" (Gen. 2.9).

Beloved, that was where God established humankind and where He wants us to be forever. God says: for I know the plans I have for you, declares the Lord, plan to prosper you and not to harm you, plan to give you hope and a future (Jer. 29: 11). He is the

Good Shepherd, who always speaks to His own; His own people hear Him and follow Him (John 10: 14). He desires to lead His own beside the still waters and restore their souls. (Ps. 23: 1 NIV)

However, these good things are not without limits. The prohibition God gave concerning the tree of life is as strong as anything we find in the commandment: "You shall not eat" (Gen. 2: 17). This stern warning was attached to the command: "for in the day that you eat the fruit of it you shall surely die" (Gen. 2: 17). Beloved, obeying God is life, and disobeying Him is death. God made it clear that fellowship with Him and partaking of God's life involves obedience. The tree became the focus of God's law, and the garden was heaven on earth. It was like a sanctuary for God's people where a husband and wife learn the wisdom of obeying Him. "The fear of the Lord is the beginning of knowledge but fools despise wisdom and discipline" (Prov. 1: 7).

Moses said, in urging the people of Israel to observe God's commandments, "Observe them carefully, for this will show your wisdom and understanding to the nations, who will hear about all those decrees and say, 'surely, this great nation is a wise and understanding people'" (Deut. 4: 6). Trust in the Lord with all your heart and lean not on your own understanding; in all your ways acknowledge him and He will make your paths straight. Do not be wise in your own eyes, fear the Lord and shun evil" (Prov. 3: 5–7). Adam was taught to fear and obey God in the garden of Eden; similarly, all humans are instructed to fear and to obey God

Beloved husbands, wives, and children, are you handling your marriages and your family lives with the fear of the Lord, or you are eating the forbidden fruit and disobeying God? You can establish your marriage and family life to replicate the marriage and family life in the garden of God if you will determine that from now on, you, your spouse, and your children will live your lives in a way that delights God, and God will surely establish the desires of your heart.

## Summation

The Gospel of John gives a detailed account of the word of God (John 1: 1–5) being revealed in human flesh as Jesus Christ (v. 14). He has been in existence with God the Father from eternity past, before creation, and actively revealed God at creation to bring all things into physical manifestation. John revealed that "Through him all things were made, without Him nothing was created that has been made. In him was life and the life was the light of men. The light shines in the darkness and the darkness has not comprehended it" (John 1: 3–5).

The same Jesus came to our world and offered himself as a living sacrifice on the cross at Calvary for our redemption. He was resurrected from death and ascended to heaven to sit at the right hand of God; He is coming back to take His own along with Him to the glorious kingdom that has no end. Jesus revealed something about this to John on the island of Patmos: "Look, he is coming with the clouds, and every eye will see him, even those who pierced him and all the peoples of the earth will mourn because of him, so shall it be Amen. I am the Alpha and the Omega says the Lord God who was, and who is to come, the Almighty" (Rev. 1: 7–8).

The Spirit of God will reveal to God's people all that must come to pass in the future. Jesus revealed further: "I am the living one, I was dead behold I am alive forever and ever and hold the key to death and Hades" (Rev. 1: 18).

There can be no argument about whether the earth and the fullness contained in them belong to the Lord, not to Satan. Unfortunately, Satan rules many homes and lives. Some of these families include born-again people who are ministering in the church, but the devil tempts them to fall into the sin of adultery and fornication. Let it be clear that these people are crucifying the Lord a second time and are giving the devil legal ground to invade their lives and send them to hell. I urge you to surrender your marriage, your lives, your children, and all that belongs to you to the Sovereign Lord, who is the beginning and the end of life. He has sole authority over eternal life; let Him rule over your marriage now and live a better legacy for future generations.

Jesus Christ declared, "I am the way, the truth and the life, no one comes to my father except through me" (John 14: 6). Jesus says that He's the eternal life God has for human; no one has access to the way and the truth outside of God's revelation in Jesus Christ. He has gone to prepare our eternal home and will return to lead us to our eternal home. He further reveals in Revelation: "Here I am! I stand at the door and knock. If anyone hears my voice and open the door, I will come in and eat with him and him with me" (Rev. 3:20). Beloved, I implore you to surrender your marriage and family to the Lord because all powers in heaven and on earth, in the sea, and under the earth belong to him alone. Let God take absolute control of your marriage and family life.

A time is fast approaching, the day of the Lord, when God will gather all the righteous people from different races, tongues, and nations to Himself. Describing this, the Bible says "Then one of the elders asked me, 'These in white robes who are they, and where did they come from?' I answered, 'Sir, you know' and he said, 'There are they who have come out of the great tribulation, they have washed their robes and made them white in the blood of the Lamb. Therefore, they are before the throne of God and serve him day and night in his temple; and he who sits on the throne will spread his tent over them. Never again will they hunger never again will they thirst. The sun will not beat upon them, or any scorching heat. For the Lamb at the centre of the throne will be their shepherd, he will lead them to springs of livings water. And God will wipe away every tear from their eyes'" (Rev. 7: 13–17). Revelation 21: 1–6 also confirms this scriptural truth. Beloved, choose to be part of the kingdom of Christ and a joint heir with the Lord by being obedient to the commandment of God for marriage.

## Pastoral Counselling

Beloved in Christ, there is no perfect man or woman on earth. Jesus Christ declared that only our Father in heaven is perfect. "Though He wants you to be perfect like His Father in heaven" (Matt. 5: 48). Don't deceive yourselves; you cannot find a perfect man or woman as a husband or wife, but with God on your side, you can turn your present partner into your perfect choice. Beloved, once you succeed in securing God's approval for your marriage, you'll have the grace and the power to turn the shortcomings of your spouse into testimonies through your prayers. Let God be the foundation of your marriage; let Him give you the ticket for your marital journey before you embark on it. He will never let you down or forsake you. If your marriage is in crisis, go on your knees and cry to Him. He will surely answer and give you testimonies of His goodness.

The current social system destroying marriages and encouraging single parents to take welfare payments is a form of slavery designed to deprive parents of moral and spiritual authority over their children. It also destroys family values and sinks the boat of marriage. While the children become rebellious and disobedient towards their parents and the society, this system also deprives them of their cultural, moral, and spiritual heritage. It has a lasting negative effect on the children, the family, the community, the nation, and the world they are living in. The social system must favour unity in marriage and family life by celebrating the couples who have succeeded in their marriages and families for twenty to sixty years and offering them benefits. They are the bedrock of a righteous nation.

If you're yearning to divorce your spouse and become a single parent, I advise you to avoid it! Rather, take your case to God in prayer for a divine intervention and solution. If you are already pursuing divorce, please stop immediately; it has the potential to affect your family life negatively and deny you eternity when practised with fornication and adultery (Gal. 5: 19–21). It violates the plan of God for humanity, in light of Him saying, "It is not good for a man to be alone" (Gen. 2: 18). I recommend changing this system to a marriage reconciliation system and promulgating laws to reduce the rate of divorce as well as rewarding couples who have managed and sustained their marriages.

Let your marriage be a seed planted in good soil, and conduct your family as an extension of the heavenly kingdom where love, truth, forgiveness, peace, and the fear of God reign for the glory of God.

> Blessed are all who fear the Lord, who walk in His ways, you will eat the fruits of you labour; blessing and prosperity will be yours. Your wife will be like a fruitful vine within your house, your sons will be

like olive shoots around your table. This is the man blessed who fears the Lord. (Ps. 128: 1–4)

## Prayers of Declaration

As mentioned earlier in this book, prayer is a weapon for Godly or Christian families; prayer is also a communication channel between man and God, initiated by the Holy Spirit in the hearts of God's people. Prayer is the electric field connecting heaven and earth; when it sparks, the matter is taken care of. The following prayer declarations are necessary for every family.

1. Father Lord, in the name of Jesus Christ, I thank you for the gift of your dear Son, Jesus Christ, who died to shed His blood on the cross for our redemption. We hereby confess our sins and declare that God is supreme and sovereign. His supreme authority rules over heaven and earth, and there is no other God beside Him.

2. Father Lord, in the name of Jesus Christ of Nazareth, we confess all the sins committed individually and collectively as husband and wife, including the sins of our parents and our ancestors. We ask for forgiveness in Jesus's name. Let the blood of our Lord atone for our sins and the power of His resurrection heal our family, in Jesus's name, amen.

3. Heavenly Father, in the name of Jesus Christ, we break ourselves loose from all generational curses; we destroy every demonic altar built by us, our parents, and our ancestors. In the name of Jesus Christ, we break ourselves loose from any dedication and covenant made at those evil altars that have been working against our destinies.

4. Father Lord, in the name of Jesus, we take the authority of the word of God, together with the power in the blood of Jesus and the anointing of the Holy Spirit, and we declare a total destruction of all demonic altars in the lineage of our fathers and mothers that may speak evil into our marriage and family. We destroy those altars with the fire of the Holy Ghost, in Jesus's name, amen.

5. Father Lord, in the name of Jesus Christ, we commit our marriage and our children into your hand for your supreme rulership. You are our God, and we submit our lives to you. We ask that you take absolute pre-eminence in our marriage and family, in Jesus's name, amen.

6. Father Lord, we immerse our marriage and our children in the blood of Jesus Christ for total cleansing from generational curses. We remove and break all yokes and burdens from our lives, in the name of Jesus Christ, amen.

7. Father Lord, let the covenant blood of the Lamb terminate and nullify every negative covenant entered into by our ancestors, our parents, and ourselves. The devil and his agents have no power over this marriage and family. We declare that such covenants are not valid and do not stand to have an effect over our lives, in Jesus's name, amen.

8. Father Lord, in the name of Jesus Christ, we declare that from today forward, we will bear fruit that lasts and fills the surface of the earth. We will succeed and prosper in all things that we do, in the name of Jesus Christ, amen.

9. Father Lord, in the name of Jesus Christ, we declare, according to your word, that no weapon fashioned against any member of this family will prosper, in the name of Jesus

Christ. Every tongue that rises against us in judgement shall be condemned, in Jesus's name, amen.

10. Father Lord, in the name of Jesus Christ, we declare that this family will be established for eternal glory; that which is little among us shall become a powerful and mighty nation. One among us shall become thousands and turn into a fountain of blessings, in the name of Jesus Christ, amen.

11. Father Lord, I plead the blood of Jesus Christ over every member of my family and declare your protection over our lives, day and night. Wherever we go, no evil shall come near us, in Jesus's name, amen.

12. Father Lord, in the name of Jesus Christ, we confess and claim that the blessing of Abraham will forever be upon the lives of our family members. We declare that no one among us will lack the good things of life, in Jesus's name, amen.

13. Father Lord, in the name of Jesus Christ, we cancel and terminate the affliction of poverty, failure, setback and stagnancy out of our family, in the name of Jesus Christ, amen.

14. Father Lord, we immerse ourselves in the blood of Jesus Christ and declare divine healing and good health upon all of our family members; wherever they go, none shall fall sick or carry any sickness or disease in their bodies, in Jesus's name, amen.

15. Father Lord, in the name of Jesus Christ of Nazareth, according to God's word at the time of creation, we claim and declare blessing, fruitfulness, and increase without

limit upon our entire family and every member of it. We send them forth to go and take dominion, according to the word of God, in Jesus's name, amen.

16. Father Lord, in the name of Jesus Christ, whatever the devil has stolen from our ancestors, our parents, and ourselves, we recover it all, in the name of Jesus Christ, amen.

17. Father Lord, in the name of Jesus Christ, none among our family members or our livestock shall be barren, in the name of Jesus Christ, amen.

18. Father Lord, in the name of Jesus Christ, give this family the grace to expand and increase southward, eastward, westward, and northward without any boundary, in the name of Jesus Christ, amen.

19. Father Lord, in the name of Jesus Christ, we declare that whosoever rises up against our family members in battle, they will fall before us a thousand times, in Jesus's name. No weapon fashioned against us will prosper, in the name of Jesus Christ, amen.

20. Father Lord, in the name of Jesus Christ and according to the word of God, we declare that none among our family members will die young or get disabled. We shall all live and fulfil our days on earth in good health, with the abundant blessing of God, in Jesus's name, amen.

21. Father Lord, in the name of Jesus Christ, we request the baptism of the Holy Spirit by fire upon all our family members. Holy Spirit, come like a rushing wind and a tongue of fire, and rest upon all our family members, old and young, in the name of Jesus Christ, amen.

22. Father Lord, in the name of Jesus Christ, let the spirit of righteousness and the fear of the Lord fill and dwell in the hearts of our family members, old and young. Give us the grace to dwell in your presence all the days of our lives, in Jesus's name, amen.

23. Father Lord, in the name of Jesus Christ, we ask for divine authority for every family member to trample upon lions and adders and to subdue the kingdom of darkness, in Jesus's name, amen.

24. Father Lord, we believe that Jesus Christ died on the cross of Calvary. We also believe in the resurrection, the ascension, and Jesus's second coming. Please, give our family the grace to wait on you in this world and to reign with you in your eternal kingdom, in the name of Jesus Christ, amen.

25. Father Lord, in the name of Jesus Christ, we ask you to visit the foundations of our family members, old and young, to destroy every foundational error and shortcoming. Purge our lives of all generational curses with the blood of the Lamb of God, in Jesus's name, amen.

### Prayers to Break All Curses

1. In the name of Jesus Christ, with the authority in the word of God and the anointing of the Holy Spirit and with the blood of Jesus Christ, I break and revoke every curse of poverty, setback, stagnancy, bitterness, barrenness, non-achievement, unfruitfulness, premature death, sickness or disease, failure or near failure that may be running in my family, back to four generations, in the name of Jesus Christ, amen.

2. I command every demonic spirit behind these curses to release me and go out of me and into the abyss, in the name of Jesus Christ. I revoke and renounce any curses pronounced against me. by witches, witchdoctors, false prophets, or other women or men, living or dead, in the name of Jesus Christ, amen.

3. I break and revoke all curses upon my life as a result of my wicked and ungodly activities in the past, in Jesus's name, amen.

4. In the name of Jesus Christ, I break and revoke all curses upon my life as a result of my immoral sexual relationships with married or unmarried persons in the past; I revoke every curse upon my life as a result of cheating widows, widowers, or orphans. I also revoke any and all curses upon my life as a result of abortions I have committed or assisted someone to commit in the past.

5. In the name of Jesus Christ, I revoke and renounce every dedication and covenant that I have made with occult groups, including witch doctors or soul ties.

6. In Jesus's name, I break and revoke any curses upon my life as a result of worshipping idols and disobedience to God; I command demons operating in my life as a result of such worship to lose their hold over my life and go to the abyss, in Jesus's name, amen.

7. In the name of Jesus Christ, I command everything that represents a curse in my life, including every mark of a curse, to be washed away with the blood of Jesus. I break every curse of failure, and I bind every spirit in charge of near success syndrome, in the name of Jesus Christ.

8. To every door of success, blessings, prosperity, favour, and breakthrough that has been closed by evil spirits behind curses, I command you to open now, in the name of Jesus Christ. I command the release of my blessings that have been delayed as a result of those curses, in Jesus's name, amen.

9. To all demonic spirits operating in me and every contact point of curses, I command you to pack your bags and come out of me now, in the name of Jesus Christ. I wipe out all evil marks of curses from my life, in the name of Jesus Christ. I establish new marks of blessing and favour, in the name of Jesus, amen.

10. I break and revoke every curse pronounced upon me by my parents, in Jesus's name. Spirits operating in my life because of parental curses, I bind you and command you to lose your hold over my life, in Jesus's name, amen.

11. I immerse myself and my family in the blood of Jesus to wash myself and my family clean from every generational curse, in the name of Jesus Christ, amen.

12. Every altars built by my ancestors for the devil, I call down fire from heaven like in the days of Elijah, let such altars be consumed by the fire of the Holy Ghost and turn them to ashes, let all the demons on assignments from those altars are bound and cast into the lake of fire in Jesus Name. Amen

**Prayers to Nullify Spiritual Marriage Covenant**

1. In the name of Jesus Christ, by the power in the blood of Jesus and the Holy Spirit and by my own will, I break the

spiritual covenant of marriage in my life for any relationship that was immoral and not ordained by God or any such relationships that were committed to by my ancestors or my parents to family deities or ancestral spirits before I was born, I break them with the covenant blood of the Lamb of God, in Jesus's name.

2. I break any spiritual covenant of marriage established by me through sexual immorality with an agent of the devil in the name of Jesus. For any spiritual marriage covenant I entered through association or involvement with occult members, witch doctors, demonic prayer houses or spiritualists, I break it with the blood of Jesus, and I divorce the spiritual wife [or husband] in Jesus's name.

3. In the name of Jesus, with the anointing of the Holy Spirit, I command everything that has entered me through sexual fantasies to come out of me now, in the name of Jesus Christ. I command every representative and point of contact with spiritual partners to come out of me now, in the name of Jesus Christ.

4. I release myself from every curse meant to hinder me from getting married or meant to break up my marriage; I break the curse now, with the blood of Jesus. For any curse by a former spiritual partner declaring that I will not get married or retain my marriage, I revoke such curse with the blood of Jesus and nullify it in the name of Jesus Christ.

5. I revoke any curse by the former spiritual partner that I will not have physical children on earth. I release my marriage from every ancestral curse and from every anti-marriage spirit, in the name of Jesus Christ. Regarding any

antimarriage spirit assigned against sons and daughters in my family, I bind them, cast them out, and send them to the lake of fire, in Jesus's name.

6. I revoke and break all marital curses placed on me by enemies of the family. I bind and command every spirit of witchcraft assigned to hinder my marriage to free your hold from my marriage, in the name of Jesus.

7. Spirits responsible for marriage dissolution and disappointment, I bind you and command you to release your hold from my marriage, in the name of Jesus Christ. Anything in me that makes prospective life partners run away from me, come out of me and go now, in the name of Jesus Christ.

8. In the Name of Jesus Christ, family deities from my mother's lineage and my father's lineage holding and delaying my marriage or causing marital misunderstanding, release me and my marital life now, in the name of Jesus Christ. From today onward, I refuse to allow any evil spirits of late marriage or marital dissolution into my family, in Jesus's name.

9. In the name of Jesus, I release myself from every curse spoken or activated by my former boyfriend [or girlfriend]. In the name of Jesus, I also command the fire of the Holy Ghost to consume and destroy anything that represents me in any coven of witches. To my intended life partner, I release you from every evil power that has hindered you from me, in the name of Jesus Christ.

10. I pray for the release of my life partner, wherever he [or she] is; begin to find me now, in the name of Jesus Christ. My

life partner, I release you from the spirit of indecision. Holy Spirit, help me to locate, recognise, and be united with my life partner, in Jesus's name.

11. Regarding every generational curse that has held my partner in bondage, I pray for the blood of the Lamb to take away the curse and set him [or her] free to locate me now, in the name of Jesus Christ, amen.

12. I ask, oh Lord, that when my life partner shall find me, you will bind us together in love, truth, honour, and respect. I request that you will honour our marriage with your blessing, prosperity, peace, and harmony, in the name of Jesus Christ, amen.

13. Father Lord, let my feet be anointed to step into the territory of my promised land. Let my hands be anointed to prosper in whatever I set them to do, in the name of Jesus Christ, amen.

14. Father Lord, I prophesy into my future that no darkness will stand against me and my family and that my family and I will be established as light to destroy every power of darkness, in Jesus's name, amen.

15. Father, I pray for baptism of fire for me and all of my family members. I ask for transcending power and the spirit of excellence to be present in me and all members of my family, in Jesus's name, amen.

## Family Diary

From the beginning of creation, throughout the history of mankind, records of family trees and genealogies have become an integral part of existence. A couple can track their lineage and the names of ancestors from both the mother's and the father's side of the family tree. This type of record can be seen in the Bible, from the record of Adam, to Noah, Abraham, and the birth of our Lord Jesus Christ. The Bible recorded forty-two generations in the genealogy of our Lord Jesus Christ.

The following pages will help you keep records of the generations in your family.

**This certifies that I,** _____

_____ **, and** _____

**Were united in holy matrimony on the** ___ **day of** _____

**By** _____

**Witness** _____

**Witness** _____

**Witness** _____

**Period of courtship** _____

**Date of engagement** _____

## Husband's Family Tree

**Husband's name** _____

**Date of birth** _____

**Place of birth** _____

**Hospital** _____ **Weight at birth** _____

**Father's name** _____

**Mother's name** _____

Parents' religious background _____

Profession _____

Name of brother _____

Name of brother _____

Name of brother _____

Name of brother _____

Name of sister _____

Name of sister _____

Name of sister _____

Grandfather's name _____

Grandmother's name _____

Grandparents' religious background _____

## Wife's Family Tree

Wife's name_____

Date of birth _____

Place of birth _____

Hospital _____ Weight at birth _____

Profession _____

Name of brother _____

Name of brother _____

Name of brother _____

Name of brother _____  _____

Name of sister _____

Name of sister _____

Name of sister _____

Grandfather's name _____

Grandmother's name _____

Grandparents' religious background _____

_____

## Children's Birth Records

Name of first child _____

_____

Date of birth _____

Hospital and place of birth _____

_____ City _____

_____

Country of birth _____

Name of second child _____

_____

Date of birth _____

Hospital and place of birth _____

_____ City _____

_____

Country of birth _____

Name of third child _____

_____

Date of birth _____

Hospital and place of birth _____

_____ City _____

_____

Country of birth _____

Name of fourth child _____

_____

Date of birth _____

Hospital and place of birth _____

_____ City _____

_____

Country of birth _____

Name of fifth child _____

_____

Date of birth _____

Hospital and place of birth _____

_____ City _____

_____

Country of birth _____

Family vision _____

_____

_____

_____

# OTHER BOOK

## *OVER THE STORMS OF LIFE,*
### *God's words and Covenant promises prevails*

# UPCOMING BOOK TITLES

1.  **GOD, and HIS KINGDOM LIFE**

2.  **THE GENESIS OF RELIGION**

3.  **HOLY SPIRIT, the abiding GOD**

4.  **VICTORY OF THE CROSS, honey from the ROCK**

# PRODUCE OF

## Kingdom Life Publications and Evangelism

**CHRIST KINGDOM (world) OUTREACH MINISTRIES**
www.christkingdomoutreach.com
pastor@christkingdomoutreach.com
pastorjoy57@gmail.com
+447950965959

*Reaching out to the world with the truth of the Gospel*
*Matthew 24:14*

*Wedding flowers, for all engaged*
*and married couples*